Philosophy of Law in Korea

When Korea began as a newly independent state in 1948, its economy was very underdeveloped, and the rule of law was just established. The journey of democratization in Korea was not without challenges. This book traces the history of the legal philosophy development in Korea and highlights Korea's unique experience. This book shows how Western legal philosophy has been accepted in Korea, a non-Western country that has newly introduced the Western legal system, and what role the legal philosophy has played in social context.

The book also examines academic scholars' intellectual activities in a historical context and how their intellectual products are yielded through their continuous response to the circumstances of the time. It specifically looks at the many challenging tasks legal philosophers had to overcome in a society when the rule of law and democracy had not yet settled. The book explores how Korean legal philosophers coped during such unique historical situations. It also illustrates how Korean scholars accepted German and Anglo-American legal philosophies and integrated them to change social realities of Korea.

Through Korea's experience, this book will provide insights into how modern legal philosophy develops in a new state and what legal philosophers' responses would be like during such a process. The developing process of legal philosophy in Korean society will interest not only readers in countries who have had similar experiences to Korea, but also readers in the West.

Jeong-Oh Kim is Professor at Law School, Yonsei University. He received B.A. and M.A. in law from Yonsei University in Korea and S.J.D. degree from University of Wisconsin-Madison. He served as the president of the Korean Association of Legal Philosophy and as the president of the Korean Association of Legal Sociology. Also, he was a dean of Yonsei Law School. He published many articles on critical legal studies and social theories of law and conducted empirical research on civil litigation and public litigation to reveal the changing trend of Korean legal culture.

Hak-Tai Kim is Professor at Law School, Hankuk University of Foreign Studies. He received Dr. iur. from University of Saarbruecken in Germany. He served as the president of the Korean Association of Legal Philosophy and as Senior

Vice President of Financial and External Affairs at Hankuk University of Foreign Studies. He published several books in Korea: *Time of Life and Human Dignity in Modern Medical Science*; *Interpretation and Application of Law*; and *Law and Truth*.

Joon-Seok Park is Professor at Law School, Jeonbuk National University. He received Ph.D. from Seoul National University and served as research director of the Korean Association of Legal Philosophy. He published several books in Korea: *Making Law Intelligible – Essays in Legal Ideas* and *The Concept of Authority*.

Dong-Ryong Shin is Professor at School of Law, Kangwon National University. He received Ph.D. from Yonsei University. He served as the general secretary of the Korean Association of Legal Philosophy. He spent a year as a visiting scholar at College of Law, Exeter University in the United Kingdom. He published articles on communitarianism, copyright, and western legal philosophy of middle age.

Routledge Studies in Asian Law

Civil Unrest and Governance in Hong Kong
Law and Order from Historical and Cultural Perspectives
Edited by Michael H.K. Ng and John D. Wong

Writing Chinese Laws
The Form and Function of Legal Statutes Found in the Qin Shuihudi Corpus
Ernest Caldwell

National Identity and Japanese revisionism
Abe Shinzō's vision of a beautiful Japan and its limits
Michal Kolmaš

Constitutional Remedies in Asia
Edited by Po Jen Yap

Chinese Legal Culture and Constitutional Order
Shiping Hua

Land Law and Disputes in Asia
In Search of an Alternative for Development
Edited by Brian Z. Tamanaha, Narufumi Kadomatsu and Yuka Kaneko

China's Foreign Investment Legal Regime
Progress and Limitations
Yuwen Li and Cheng Bian

Philosophy of Law in Korea
Acceptance, Engagement and Social Change
Jeong-Oh Kim, Hak-Tai Kim, Joon-Seok Park, Dong-Ryong Shin

For more information about this series, please visit: www.routledge.com/asian studies/series/RSIAL

Philosophy of Law in Korea

Acceptance, Engagement and Social Change

Jeong-Oh Kim, Hak-Tai Kim, Joon-Seok Park and Dong-Ryong Shin

Routledge
Taylor & Francis Group
LONDON AND NEW YORK

First published 2023
by Routledge
4 Park Square, Milton Park, Abingdon, Oxon OX14 4RN

and by Routledge
605 Third Avenue, New York, NY 10158

Routledge is an imprint of the Taylor & Francis Group, an informa business

British Library Cataloguing-in-Publication Data
A catalogue record for this book is available from the British Library

ISBN: 978-0-367-74178-5 (hbk)
ISBN: 978-0-367-74179-2 (pbk)
ISBN: 978-1-003-15643-7 (ebk)

DOI: 10.4324/9781003156437

Typeset in Galliard
by Apex CoVantage, LLC

Contents

Acknowledgments

This book is based on papers from *The Forming and Unfolding of Contemporary Legal Philosophy in Korea*, published in Korea in 2010. The authors have significantly revised the previous papers and included new content. We are deeply indebted to members of the Korean Association of Legal Philosophy, who actively supported the book's publication. We are grateful to Yongling Lam, who strongly supported the book's inclusion in the Routledge Focus Series.

We are also deeply grateful to Joe Phillips for his time and effort to smooth our English text. He currently is a Yonsei University professor teaching philosophical foundations of law and social justice, among other courses. Having lived in Korea for several decades, he has considerable knowledge of the country's modern history.

Introduction

Jeong-Oh Kim

1 Understanding the Philosophy of Law

Philosophies of law are formed in mature civilizations. Western traditions are grounded in the two great pillars of natural law theory and legal positivism. Eastern legal philosophies contain similar thoughts but also many differences. Confucianism and Legalism in the East, which mirror the opposition between natural law theory and legal positivism,[1] diverge over the role of legal rules, and each has occupied a dominant position at different points in Korean history. For example, during the Joseon Dynasty (1392–1910), Korea's pre-modern era, Confucianism dominated and profoundly influenced Koreans' thoughts and behaviors. By the mid-twentieth century, the modern Western legal system began to supplement Confucianism, raising the question: What role has the philosophy of law played in this transition? Before addressing that question, I will briefly explain the terms used in this book.

Unlike common law countries, 'jurisprudence' is not widely used in Korea. William Twining points out that in the Anglo-American tradition, jurisprudence, legal theory, and philosophy of law each refer to academic studies dealing with theoretical questions at a relatively high level of abstraction.[2] Jurisprudence and legal theory are synonyms, and "in this view, jurisprudence is the theoretical part of law as a discipline with several jobs or functions to perform to contribute to its health." Legal philosophy is one part of jurisprudence that addresses "theories of justice, questions of metaphysics, epistemology, or meta-ethics."[3] However, as Professor H.L.A. Hart acknowledged,[4] it is not easy to distinguish among the three terms. In Korean legal academia, legal philosophy has been used to encompass jurisprudence, legal theory, and legal philosophy. Accordingly, our authors use 'legal philosophy' as an inclusive term like jurisprudence.

Since Hart's theoretical framework,[5] Western legal philosophers have hotly debated how to understand the philosophy of law. On the one hand, it is viewed as a general theory applicable to any society with a modern legal system; while, on the other hand, it is understood as forming and developing according to each society's tradition and evolution. Twining labels the former "general jurisprudence" and the latter "particular jurisprudence."[6] Applying Hart's framework, which takes the generalist position, it may be possible to trace the formation of

DOI: 10.4324/9781003156437-1

the primary and secondary rules, including the rule of recognition, in Korea's modern legal system. Employing Professor Ronald Dworkin's theory,[7] which takes the particularistic position, we can explore the realization and development of political morality in the modern Korean legal system. Philosophy of law's direct and active impact during Korea's dramatically changing modern legal history provides a distinctive perspective on these debates.

Twining suggests a new perspective[8] addressing the criticism that jurisprudence, which formed and developed in the West, is parochial and ethnocentric.[9] Regarding the relationship between the new brand of 'global jurisprudence' and general jurisprudence, he suggests the following:

> The central argument is that our discipline in this quite local sense needs to become more genuinely cosmopolitan and to broaden its perspective both geographically and intellectually. From a global perspective our predominant traditions of academic law have focused mainly on the domestic municipal law of modern nation states, have assumed that doctrine is the core of the subject matters of the discipline, and have tended toward universalism and secularism in respect of values despite the phenomena of belief pluralism and religious revival. Collectively we have generally been ignorant of other legal traditions and belief systems and generally indifferent to legal phenomena and problems in other parts of the world. My argument is not that our discipline should abandon its local roots and its concern with immediate detailed practical problems, but rather that building on the strengths of our heritage it should broaden its vision to include other levels of ordering, other forms of law, understanding of other legal traditions and belief systems, and to engage more with pressing global and transnational issues.[10]

He proposes that, to break free from the limitations of modern Western jurisprudence, a general jurisprudence fully embracing non-Western societies' stories, especially Southern voices, should be constructed from the perspective of globalization. In particular, he deals with human rights as an important topic in globalization. His argument raises questions: How problematical is parochialism when applying the modern Western legal system to non-Western countries? Should we conclude that Western jurisprudence is parochial merely because it was formed in the West?

Through examining the establishment, development, and operation of the philosophy of law during Korea's modern history, the authors present a new perspective on the issues posed by Twining. This introduction begins that study with a brief description of how Western legal philosophical thoughts developed in the Korean social context.

2 Korea's Modern History

Korea, which had been under Japanese colonial rule for thirty-six years, was liberated at the end of World War II in 1945.[11] However, the Korean Peninsula was divided at the thirty-eighth parallel between North Korea, ruled by the Soviet Union, and South Korea, governed by the United States. Though both Koreas later established independent governments, the division continues. This situation is not merely the coexistence of two countries with different identities, ideologies, and places in the international system, but a very unstable situation with the ever-present risk of military confrontation.

The Korean people wished to establish a modern state, not restore the pre-colonial Joseon Dynasty. This process began with the March First Movement, a nationwide non-violent protest against Japanese colonial rule in 1919, and the provisional government's establishment in Shanghai, China, which created an opportunity for a modern, non-monarchial state.[12]

Before the three years of US military rule ended, South Korea's Constitutional Assembly was created through a modern referendum on May 10, 1948, the first Constitution was promulgated, and the Assembly elected the president, establishing the Korean government (First Republic). The People's Republic of Korea was founded in the North on September 9, 1948.

Just two years later, the Korean War broke out with North Korea's invasion and attempted unification of the Korean Peninsula under a communist government. Closely following decades of Japanese colonialism, the war imposed great hardships on Koreans, destroying all major industrial facilities in the South and inflicting incalculable casualties. After the 1953 armistice, the Korean government was tasked with recovery from colonialism and the war. Although the South's government was based on its modern Constitution, the public maintained a traditional Confucian consciousness and lifestyle, making the political, social, and economic situations difficult to change and weakening the rule of law.[13]

Public antipathy increased due to the corruption of politicians and bureaucrats surrounding Rhee Syngman,[14] who had held the presidency since 1948. On April 19, 1960, protests, led by young students, broke out in major cities against Rhee's March 1960 fraudulent re-election, leading to his resignation. Following the April Revolution, the Constitution was amended to replace the presidential system with a cabinet government and a bicameral legislature (Second Republic). A general election was then held, and a new government was established under this Constitution. A free, active media arose, and the public enjoyed a liberal polity.

As regulations were lifted, accumulated demands from all walks of life simultaneously erupted. The public demanded punishment for past government corruption, including punishing the culprits behind election fraud during the Rhee regime. Due to an economic downturn since the end of the 1950s, the unemployed reached 2.4 million at the end of 1960, and 80% of the factories in the Seoul region were shut down. Some two million farmers found themselves on the verge of starvation that spring.[15] The military was most sensitive to the social chaos, economic instability, and government's apparent ineffectiveness.

On May 16, 1961, a military coup by young officers led by Major General Park Chung-Hee overthrew the democratic regime of the Second Republic. The Supreme Council for National Reconstruction, a military administration, was established as the governing body. In December 1962, the military government revised the Constitution, returning to a presidential system and unicameral National Assembly (Third Republic); it promised to transfer the government to a civil administration within two years. In October 1963, a presidential election was held under the new Constitution, with Park Chung-Hee, the coup's leader, elected president.

Park Chung-Hee's government pursued a strong state-led growth policy with the slogans of economic firstism and modernization of the homeland, goals that justified political oppression and injustice. The basic direction of economic policy was nurturing industry by introducing foreign capital and technology, exporting products using high-quality, cheap labor, and accumulating capital – an export-led economic development. During the 1960s and 1970s, annual exports increased by an average of 29% and economic growth by 8.9%, leading many to regard Korea's development model as the best among developing countries.[16] This growth emphasized national identity, boosted people's pride, and reflected President Park's strong belief in a 'just do it' approach where a development dictatorship played a large leadership role.

However, the Constitution limited the president to three terms, so Park Chung-Hee, who was serving his third term, and his political allies declared emergency martial law in October 1972, disbanded the National Assembly, and enacted the so-called Yushin Constitution at an emergency meeting of the State Council. A referendum confirmed the new Constitution in November (Fourth Republic). It created a new sovereign body – the National Council for Unification Subjects – to indirectly elect the president, removed the term limit, and allowed the president to control the parliament and the judiciary, thereby guaranteeing indefinite presidential authority. In 1978, Park was re-elected president, and in the National Assembly elections the opposition party won the popular vote but remained in the minority. At the end of May 1979, Kim Young-Sam, who was elected leader of the opposition party, actively struggled for democracy; in October of that year, the National Assembly expelled him. This incident triggered public condemnation at home and abroad, with a large-scale resistance movement arising in southeastern cities and spreading nationwide. The government was at a crossroads; either it could accede to these demands for reform or suppress the uprising with military force. Amid this instability, President Park was assassinated by the head of the Korean Central Intelligence Agency on October 26. This marked the end of the eighteen-year Park Chung-Hee era.

The people expected the Yushin regime and military rule to end, but another military coup in December 1979 replaced Park, sparking a large-scale student demonstration in May 1980. The new military government declared martial law, halted all political activities, posted armed soldiers in the universities, and arrested major politicians, including opposition leader Kim Young-Sam, labeling them power-hoarders. Shortly thereafter, when excessive martial law resulted in many casualties in Gwangju City, students and Gwangju citizens seized weapons and waged a street fight against the army. Protests spread to nearby areas. Martial law forces suppressed the resistance and restored order in Gwangju on May 27, but the tragic wounds resulting from the two hundred civilian deaths did not heal easily. A new military government amended the Constitution so that a presidential electoral college indirectly elected the president to a single seven-year term (Fifth Republic). In February 1981, Chun Doo-Hwan was elected under the new system as the twelfth president.

From the mid-1980s, the democratization movement spread among students, politicians, and all walks of life. Student demonstrations became increasingly violent and included occupying the ruling party's headquarters and several cases of self-immolation and other suicides. In January 1987, an incident sparked a national democratic uprising. Amid rising public outrage over the death of a university student during police torture, President Chun banned all discussions on the constitutional amendment. On June 10, after another university student was shot and killed by police during a protest, the demonstrations spread across the country. More than a million people participated, including students, politicians, and civilians. On June 29, the government announced eight articles, including a constitutional amendment for a direct presidential election (Sixth Republic). A referendum confirmed the amendment in October 1987; a presidential election was held on December 16; and the president was directly elected for the first time since 1971.[17]

Constitutional legitimacy was nearly restored by the 1987 Constitution, which addressed major public demands and dramatically departed from previous constitutions that were institutionalized through coups or unusual means to perpetuate the ruling powers. At its heart is the direct election of a president, who serves a single five-year term. It also strengthens the Assembly's authority and further protects individual rights. In 1992, a civilian president, Kim Young-Sam, who had fought authoritarian regimes all his adult life, was elected. This watershed moment singled the transfer from military-based power to public-based civilian power.[18]

In the 1997 election, Kim Dae-Jung, a life-long dissident and leader of the opposition party, was successful in his fourth attempt to become president. This was the first transfer of power to the opposition party in Korea's modern history.

The 1987 Constitution introduced a European constitutional court system. The Constitution of the Second Republic (1960–1961) included provisions to establish a constitutional court, but, unfortunately, the court was aborted due to the 1961 military coup. Thus, this Constitutional Court is the first one implemented in Korean constitutional history.

This Court has jurisdiction over (1) the constitutionality of laws, (2) the impeachment of high officials, including the president, (3) the dissolution of political parties engaging in unconstitutional purposes, (4) intragovernmental jurisdictional controversies, and (5) adjudicating constitutional petitions – the Korean equivalent of the German *Verfassungsbeschwerde*.[19] As a result, democracy and the rule of law began to operate. Particularly, with a legally established Constitutional Court, the government's unconstitutional actions started to be restricted.

3 Philosophy of Law in a Social Context

Research and debate in legal philosophy, which is ongoing in Western academia, is often conducted at a distance from reality. However, in countries where democracy and the rule of law have not been properly established, legal philosophical arguments have sometimes emerged as powerful weapons in the process of trials or resistance.

Although Korea's modern Constitution was enacted in 1948 and the government was based on it, the situation has been very different from that in Western countries where established constitutionalism and legal systems have long existed. In Korea, we see a direct use of legal philosophical arguments in some cases. Among the major pillars of Western legal philosophy – natural law theory and legal positivism – the former played an active role. Several cases reveal how those legal philosophical arguments have been asserted in the social context of Korea's modern history.[20]

Upon the outbreak of the Korean War in 1950, the South Korean government issued an emergency order titled "*The Special Ordinance for Measuring the Specified Crimes under the Emergency Period*."[21] The main contents were the death penalty, life imprisonment, and fixed-term imprisonment of more than ten years for serious and general crimes during wartime.[22] The South's government, which had retreated to the southeast due to North Korea's invasion, applied this order after retaking Seoul in September of that year. The judges presiding in those cases were in a very difficult situation. Some persons standing trial had actively sympathized with the North Korean army during its rule and harmed neighbors, but other cases were debatable. For example, responding to the prosecutor's request for punishment, Judge Byung-Jin Yoo acquitted two teenagers charged with entering an evacuated police official's home and stealing two bottles of liquor and daily necessities after they saw North Korean soldiers exiting the house with several household items. Judge Yoo wrote:

> I cannot but feel the gap between the law and reality is too large to impose that heavy sentence. If I am truly bound by the law to the point of becoming a slave to the law, then I must leave the office of judge. Thus, these concerns again lead to resolving the large gap between the purpose of the trial and compliance with the law. However, in this case . . . is it a disregard of the law? No. Rather than disregarding the law, it is the creation of a norm through a trial. So, I boldly and without hesitation acquitted him.[23]

Judge Yoo described his conception of the law:

> The view that, no matter how bad a law may be, if it is not respected . . . society will be in chaos and order cannot be maintained, is exaggerated. . . . In general, when can a law, whose main purpose is to defend justice and truth, betray that justice and serve only its ultimate purpose, legal stability? We have to make a clear distinction between the principal and the

> auxiliary. . . . If you are a jurist based on justice, or if you are a legal practitioner who claims to be a defender of justice, wouldn't it be impossible to follow these laws blindly? Yes. Even if it is a law, as long as it opposes the truth, we must fight against it. And you must live the truth. Nevertheless, what was our attitude in the past? Since we were afraid of the argument that an 'Evil law is also law,' did we just follow it by bowing our heads?[24]

Judge Yoo, who was in a position to apply the harsh law during a terrible wartime, instead relied on a legal conception very similar to natural law theory to reject its application in the teenagers' case.

The 1972 Yushin Constitution empowered the president to promulgate urgent orders limiting basic rights, especially freedoms of speech and assembly. Poet Ji-Ha Kim's 1975 *Declaration of Conscience*, written while imprisoned for anti-government activity, drew on Thomas Aquinas' natural law thought as a basis for resisting the dictatorship:

> In Catholic political thought after Thomas Aquinas, it has been recognized that the people themselves are clearly given the right and duty in natural law to overthrow the obvious tyrannical oppression that violates the survival of the people and infringes on the common good. This causes a sudden universal awakening of the people and a miracle leap in history by creating an explosive turning point in which the people themselves restored their humanity, which was lost from oppression.[25]

In 1974, a defense attorney, Shin-Ok Kang, defended students prosecuted for violating an emergency decree. He argued in a court pleading: "Law is a maid of political power. This trial is judicial murder committed by exploiting law. People do not need to follow an unjust law and can resist and struggle against those bad laws."[26] As a result of these arguments, Kang was sentenced to ten years in prison and suspended from legal practice for ten years for violating emergency decrees and contempt of court. In the appellate trial, Kang argued in his letter supporting the appeal, entitled "Cannot be Punished for the Defense of the Defense Attorney":

> In the field of law, what kind of law binds people to obey the laws? There are two kinds of laws, just law and unjust law. Only just laws can bind people. People have no obligation to abide by unjust laws, and they have a right to resist unjust laws. There is a confrontation between two views on this problem, natural law theory and positivist theory. . . . In any case, I believe that, in the philosophy of law, the theories of natural law prevail at present.[27]

He pointed out ten theoretical reasons why the emergency decrees were against rational and natural law, and asked the court to adjudicate his belief that, applying natural law, those laws were evil, no longer law, and need not be followed. Regarding his status and protection as the defendants' attorney, Kang cited arguments and precedents from prominent jurists in England and the Continental countries, along with the theories of Aristotle, Thomas Aquinas, John Locke, and Gustav Radbruch, among others.

In the 1980s, natural law theory became popular among students and intellectuals, who supported the democratization movement, and natural rights were recognized as justifying the right to resist authoritarian regimes. In the case addressing the assassination of President Park Chung-Hee, the Supreme Court held that "even if the argument that the existence of the right to resistance is recognized, as long as the right of resistance is not based on positive law but only on natural law, a judge cannot invoke it as a rule of law."[28] However, the minority opinion argued:

> Even if the right to resistance is not stipulated in the Constitution, it is reasonable to recognize the right to resist positive statutes that violate the human rights of the people and disturb the basic democratic order as a kind of right based on natural law. If this right of resistance were recognized, there would be no reason to exclude its function as a judicial norm.[29]

In 1987, the Constitution was amended through a vote by the National Assembly and a national referendum, marking a turning point for Korean democracy and the rule of law. Since then, the most intense legal debates have occurred in 1995 and 1996. After President Park Chung-Hee passed away in 1979, there was an active movement to enact laws to punish those who took part in the coup led by President Chun Doo-Hwan and his subordinates. The public prosecutor and legal scholars, including legal philosophers, fiercely debated the proposed laws.

The public prosecutor announced that if a coup succeeded and a new legal order was established through the people's approval (a referendum, presidential election, etc.), the new legal order would become the effective law, and the coup would no longer be a rebellion or subject to judicial review. The public prosecutor insisted that "judicial cases have not yet determined whether a series of actions to create a new government and constitutional order in the political reform process are subject to judicial review, but their legal justification could be recognized where a new constitutional order is established after a successful national political judgment."[30] The prosecutor presented arguments based on Georg Jellinek's theory of the normative force of facts, the legal philosopher Hun-Sup Shim's theory, Hans Kelsen's concept of *Grundnorm*, and Gustav Radbruch's argument on legal stability. In response, Hun-Sup Shim published an article that thoroughly analyzed the prosecutor's arguments and revealed how they distorted and misused those legal philosophies. He concluded that, from a legal philosophical point of view, the prosecutor's decision could be viewed only as an "unsuccessful decision" based on the jurisprudence of a successful coup.[31]

The Constitutional Court accepted the arguments of legal scholars and held that justification for a rebellion should be determined based on its objective content according to "whether it contains values such as the realization of justice, breaking of injustice, protection of the liberal democratic basic order, restoration of national sovereignty, etc."[32] The Court's judgment was developed and elaborated in a decision by the Seoul High Court a year later in the appellate trial of the case of 5.18 Gwangju Democratization Movement. That court made clear that de facto impunity for the coup actors is neither approval nor immunity from criminality and then opined:

> If behind or above the Constitution, there is a universal principle of law that contains the principles of justice, goodness, and peace, which is called natural law. Only constitutional provisions and legal norms that conform to these natural laws have legitimacy. Natural law is immutable, but its perception differs depending on the degree of enlightenment through human reason. Thus, when a perception prevails in a society that the constitution or basic legal order is unjust and contrary to natural law, and a drastic struggle to overcome the inconsistency by force develops, it is called a revolution.[33]

During Korea's dictatorship and authoritarianism periods after the modern Constitution was enacted in 1948, legal philosophical arguments appeared to operate actively and directly in the trial process. Even though such cases have occurred intermittently, the ripple effect has been great. While a legal positivist argument is not specifically expressed in cases, it can be seen as inherently presupposed in the adjudication process. Looking at these processes, we observe that in countries that received the West's modern legal system, the legal philosophical thought underlying that system has been accepted in parallel. Of course, philosophical thinking works differently depending on a society's nature and evolutionary process.

4 Reception of Continental and Anglo-American Legal Philosophies

Although the study of legal philosophy can use philosophical methods to explore whether the law should pursue and establish ideas as universal concepts, this study cannot be separated from the local social reality or legal practice because its objects are norms formed in the society. Furthermore, since ideas on law must face social reality, the philosophy of law cannot remain only a science, and legal philosophical inquiry must evolve to respond to a legal reality that is constantly changing through the flows of time and place.

Chapter 1 of this book describes the development of Korean legal philosophy after 1945. Dong-Ryong Shin and Jeong-Oh Kim divide the ensuing decades into four periods and describe each period's social context and specific legal philosophy. The first period is from 1945, when the country was liberated from Japanese colonial rule, to 1960, when the Second Republic was born. The political, social, and economic situations were very unstable. The Korean War, which broke out in 1950, devastated the country and indelibly scarred the people. Shin and Kim explain how Korean legal philosophy took root under these difficult conditions. During this time, Korean legal scholars deliberated on teaching and studying Western legal philosophy in Korean universities. In particular, they sought to break from the viewpoints of Japanese academics, who had taught them the philosophy of law.

The second period covers 1960 to the beginning of the Sixth Republic in 1987. A democratic government was established with the April Revolution in 1960, but, in less than a year, a military coup created an authoritarian government, which continued until 1987. Looking at the characteristics of Korean legal philosophy in this political situation, Shin and Kim point out that this was a dark age for natural law, and blind legal positivism became the mainstream. Remarkable research was published, including an empirical study examining the gap between Korea's newly enacted modern legal system, modeled on Western legal systems, and the country's unique traditional legal culture. A second work was a theoretical search to understand Korea's unique tradition and for an ethical principle that combined Eastern and Western philosophical thoughts. Shin and Kim describe the political situation in Korea during the 1960s and 1970s, the process of forming the authoritarian system, and what legal actions were taken. In the wake of the April Revolution, Korean legal philosophers were interested in natural law theories, especially the right of resistance, and began to study those theories. Students who studied in Germany deepened their research on natural law theory, especially on Radbruch's legal theory. But an incident in 1967 – the so-called East Berlin-North Korean spy ring – deterred them from actively publishing their research.

However, the democracy movement continued, and in the mid-1970s the Yushin Constitution was openly criticized by religious leaders based on natural law. However, the judiciary rejected a right of resistance based on natural law theory.

Shin and Kim review articles published by two legal scholars in the 1960s. Pyong-Choon Hahm revealed the uniqueness of Korean traditional culture and compared it to Western legal culture. He characterized it as an alegalistic attitude deeply rooted in Korean history and Koreans' consciousness. Thus, Hahm indicated that a large gap between the transplanted Western legal system and Korean traditions is inevitable. He argued that this gap must be narrowed to modernize Korean society and develop its economy.

Unlike Hahm, Hang-Nyeong Yi tried to combine Eastern and Western thought in terms of Korea's unique concept of *pungto. Pungto* refers to a particular area's geographical conditions, like climate and the shape of the land. Yi argued that *pungto* determines people's personality and a country's customs, institutions, and traditions, including its legal forms. Based upon *pungto*, he suggested the ethical principles of *gikbun* that have governed Korean life for a long time. Shin and Kim describe Yi's *punto* theory and point out that, while possessing originality, it is very difficult to apply to modern society.

In addition to these cultural studies, Shin and Kim notice an important change in legal positivism. Hun-Sup Shim, a leading legal philosopher of his time, was known as a legal positivist and criticized for not responding to Korea's unjust, tyrannical political situation. Shim responded that his theory is critical legal positivism, which recognizes that the legal system must guarantee human rights and peaceful order. Positive law should ensure this minimum, and legislators and executors should secure it.

The third period is from the 1987 civil revolution to the mid-1990s, when Korean legal philosophy rapidly developed. Several papers on natural law, human dignity, and democracy were published; legal philosophers became actively involved in the debate on social issues; new academic movements arose; research on law and society began; and a research group expressing the progressive left formed. This section describes those developments in the social context and the research's specific features. This was the most intense period in Korean society and for Korean legal scholars. Natural law theory was vigorously argued around 1987 and, unlike before, actively promoted by legal scholars. Their articles were not merely academic but aimed to reflect on and reform Korea's concrete legal reality. They prioritized universal human rights and democracy rather than a Korean-style democracy. The most in-depth study and publication of natural law theory was by Zai-Woo Shim, who emphasized human dignity by combining Eastern and Western philosophies. During this period, Korean academia's most significant characteristic was the active participation by legal scholars in social transformation movements. Shin and Kim describe these activities, especially those unfolding based on the sociology of law. The scholars' main purpose was abolishing laws suppressing the rights and lives of Korean citizens.

One event in 1994 signified the decisive role of legal philosophy during Korea's democratic transformation. A serious question arose about whether former presidents could be held legally responsible and punished for violently suppressing the 1980 Gwangju uprising. Shin and Kim describe this issue in detail and explain Korean legal philosophers' response and the court's incorporation of their arguments.

During the fourth period, from the mid-1990s to the present, democracy and institutional systems guaranteeing basic rights stabilized, and remarkable research appeared. Theoretical works sought to converge legal positivism and natural law theory and suggest an institutional natural law theory. A study on changes in civil litigation revealed Korea's rapidly evolving legal culture and transformation from a traditional legal society to a litigious one. Legal philosophy studies began to shift from the macro-level to micro-level. Before 1987, Korean legal philosophers primarily sought to realize democratization and aimed their studies at macroscopic institutional change. Recent works deal with methodologies of judicial arguments and various social issues.

Until the early 1990s, Korean legal philosophers offered limited answers to new social issues, but this gradually changed during the fourth period. As democracy began to take hold, various social problems arose, which legal philosophers did not have sufficient theoretical foundations to address. These philosophers, particularly young ones, diversified their research topics and actively responded to social changes. Shin and Kim describe the resulting philosophical evolution where natural law and legal positivism converge and institutional and anthropological natural law advance.

During the 1960s, Korean legal scholars worried about the large gap between Korea's traditional culture and modern legal system, and they devoted themselves to a solution. However, in the 1990s, several scholars found that civil litigation in Korea was comparable to that in the United States. These findings revealed Koreans' adaptation to, and active use of, the modern legal system developed since 1948. Shin and Kim detail these turns toward researching the judicial system and diverse socio-political topics.

In Chapter 2, Hak-Tai Kim traces German legal philosophy after 1945 and Korean legal scholars' acceptance of the changing trend. German jurists, who experienced the Nazi regime, returned to a natural law theory, concluding that legal positivism, the mainstream in early twentieth-century German thought, had inherent limitations that could not prevent the Nazi's extreme legalism. Koreans, who experienced Japanese imperialism, identified with these views. In particular, Gustav Radbruch's Formula of *Gesetzlich Unrecht und übergesetzliches Recht*, which influenced many trials after World War II, ushered in a natural law renaissance in the 1950s–1960s.

However, Hart and Norbert Hörster criticized Radburch's formula. Kim elaborates on these arguments and suggests that they can be refuted. Radbruch did not deny positive law; he recognized its legal status. However, positive law can exceed the boundaries of 'justice,' which we conceptually clarify by consulting the general consensus – a universal moral sensibility about what is just and unjust. For example, we can decide that laws allowing concentration camps, slavery, genocide, sex trafficking, and discrimination based on race, origin, and gender are unjust. Some philosophers criticize this 'justice' standard as so abstract that it violates a basic principle of criminal law – "without law, there is no crime, and, without law, there is no punishment" (*nulla poena sine lege*). Kim responds that the actor need not know that the written law prohibits the specific behavior; it is sufficient for the actor to recognize that the conduct was against the norm's essential meaning because it was unjustified and harmful in light of relevant social and ethical values.

Kim provides an in-depth description of natural law theory developed by German legal philosophers during the 1960s and 1970s. In particular, he discusses natural law theories, paying attention to Artur Kaufman's attempt to combine natural law with historicity and harmonize absolutism and relativity, validity and becoming, immutability and development, and eternity and historicity. Kim suggests that this harmony is the basic structure of the law, the polarity of natural and positive law, and the existence between essence and *Dasein*.

Kim then discusses Germany's border guard cases (*mauerschützfall*). Before the country's reunification, East German security guards fired on thousands attempting to escape over the Berlin Wall, killing or injuring many. After unification, the question arose whether to punish the guards, and German jurists thought that the issue was very similar to that surrounding the prosecution of Nazis after World War II. The German Federal Court ruled that the East German security law violated justice. However, Kim argues that the Nazi comparison and Radbruch's 'justice' standard seem inappropriate because the genocide of Jews was carried out at the national level, while the provision for firing at unauthorized border crossings was the subject of domestic debate.

As natural law discourses diminished and legal methodology took center stage in the 1970s, German legal philosophy tended to move from a value theory to an analytical study and from the philosophy of law to the study of legal theory. Regarding German legal methodology, Kim traces the process from nineteenth-century conceptual jurisprudence to object jurisprudence, profit jurisprudence, and free law theory. He describes the main characteristics of each school. Regarding methodologies of legal interpretation, Kim argues that legal interpretation occurs not only through formal and logical explanation under the assumption of strict literary interpretation and a closed system of law premised on the completeness and integrity of the law's existence. Rather, this interpretation also considers the law's ideas and value, the proper proposition as a moral principle, and social reality.

Korean legal philosophy began to accept these changes in German thought. During the 1950s, legal philosophers who had studied under Japanese professors during colonial rule tended to rely on Hans Kelsen's theory. However, in the 1960s, Korean students studying in Germany and writing doctoral theses on Gustav Radbruch's legal philosophy introduced his work and advanced their research. As the number of Radbruch scholars increased, his theory became important in Korean legal academia. Kim points out that, just as Radbruch's theory helped solve problems arising from the trials of Nazi war criminals, it played a key role in liquidating the legacy of Japanese colonial rule and Korea's thirty-year military dictatorship. From the 1970s, Korean legal philosophers turned to Germany's revival of natural law theory, and some scholars published papers introducing the topic.

In the 1980s and 1990s, Korean legal philosophers turned to German legal philosophers' new natural law theory and published many papers to restore a healthy legal philosophy, which 1970s–1980s authoritarian regimes had suppressed and distorted. Korean legal philosophers concentrated on topics including the theory of justice, human rights, democracy, the limits and legitimacy of state power, and the right to resist dictatorship.

Though some Korean scholars introduced legal methodology found in 1970s German legal philosophy, it was not actively explored. In the 1990s, as young scholars retuned from studies in Germany, contemporary German legal theories were actively disseminated. In particular, these philosophers accepted the dialogue theory of Habermas and Alexy. Their deep interest in legal methodology led to a fierce debate over the Korean Supreme Court's interpretation of a criminal law statute. Kim details this controversy.

In the final part of Chapter 2, Kim compares Korea and Germany's legal regulation of bioethics. As an expert in bioethics who has published many papers in this field in Korea, he focuses on how the law should respond to problems arising from biotechnology's rapid development. In particular, he analyzes the similarities and differences in the two countries' legal rules and jurisprudence. Kim first describes biotechnology's development from the 1950s to the present. He points out the need for additional ethical and legal regulations to address human cloning through implanting a cloned embryo in the womb.

Kim traces Germany's legislation. Its first bioethical law, enacted in 1990, protected embryos and emphasized human dignity. Considered too rigid, the law was amended in 2002 to permit embryonic stem cell research, but it prohibits, in principle, using embryonic stem cells to generate income and acquiring stem cells to create embryos in Germany. Korea classifies human embryos as potential human beings who gain legal status as fully human while developing, and it prohibits creating an embryo for treatment studies.

Kim argues that, while Korean legal philosophy actively monitors and accompanies German thought, twenty-first-century Korean legal philosophy should not incorporate foreign theories merely to serve philosophical universality. It should consider whether the discourse suits Korea's legal climate and expand into areas relevant to Korean culture.

In Chapter 3, Joon-Seok Park describes Korea's acceptance of Anglo-American jurisprudence. Korean jurists became interested in the American legal system during the United States' 1945–1948 military rule. They thought that by familiarizing themselves with Anglo-American law as the counterpart to civil law, which they already understood, they could create a more complete, balanced legal order. However, after major positive laws were enacted under the civil law system during the 1960s, jurists and legal scholars' main interest became investigating the civil law system, especially Germany's legal system. Of course, some Anglo-American legal philosophers' books were translated, and several published articles introduced their theories.

Park highlights criminal law as a unique case where Korea's modern legal system accepts traditional norms. Article 20 of the Criminal Act stipulates that behavior that does not violate social norms is not punishable. Interpreting this law, the Supreme Court explained that even when an action seems to be criminalized conduct, it is not illegal and cannot be punished if considered an extremely normal form of life and within the scope of the historically created order of social life. Park describes the reasoning behind this regulation: After South Korea became a newly independent republic, legislators intended to preserve social norms inherited from the country's traditional modus vivendi while encouraging progress toward a modern standard of living. However, combining Korea's modern legal system and traditional norms can render legal judgments very difficult.

There were some very important academic achievements in the 1960s and 1970s. Park discusses the pioneering works of two legal scholars, Paul Ryu and Pyong-Choon Hahm, who studied in the United States and taught students in Korea. They were interested in the large gap between Korea's transplanted legal system and traditional legal culture.

Paul Ryu, a criminal law scholar and legal philosopher, tried to build a unique theory based on linguistic symbolism and depth psychology. The former relates to laws and legal concepts put in a linguistic form, while the latter primarily concerns persons to whom the law applies. His attempt seemed very strange to his colleagues, who approached legal cases from a conceptual analysis. The methodology that Ryu learned from the neo-legal realists astonished contemporary Korean legal scholars.

Pyong-Choon Hahm employed empirical methodology to investigate the legal consciousness of the Korean people. Although this methodology was not unfamiliar to colleagues, his approach was not popular in legal academia. Park indicates that empirical legal research does not rest simply on the doctrinal analysis of positive sources of law, nor secondary sources. It requires collecting and analyzing first-hand data, designing a research structure for testing or generating a hypothesis, and, finally, constructing a quantitative or qualitative methodology. This contrasts with the lack of reflection on methodological considerations characteristic of traditional legal research. Park describes the significance of Hahm's empirical inquiry: Korea was an ideal laboratory for empirical studies of law seeking to discover discrepancies between law in books and law in action, or between what the law says and what law does, because it received modern rules of law while maintaining traditional social norms. Hahm directed his attention to this gap between the imported official law and traditional legal culture. Park concludes that Hahm's contribution is no longer considered small. He was no ordinary black-letter man but a man of the future.

Park divides the development of British legal philosophy into five stages. First, the medieval legal philosophy of John Duns Scotus and William of Ockham; second, seventeenth-century legal philosophy led by Thomas Hobbes and John Locke's theories of natural rights; third, William Blackstone's eighteenth-century legal philosophy; fourth, Jeremy Bentham, John Austin, and John Stuart Mill's nineteenth-century utilitarian legal philosophies and Albert Venn Dicey's liberal legal philosophy; and fifth, the twentieth-century legal philosophy centering on H.L.A. Hart's analytical approach.

Park reviews Korean legal philosophers' published articles on the development of British legal philosophy. He points out that they insufficiently study British medieval philosophy of law; they have not expanded Locke's theories compared to the great German philosophers, and research on Bentham as an analytical jurist remains nascent.

After reviewing the acceptance of British legal philosophy, Park traces the reception of American jurisprudence. In the 1950s and 1960s, many of Rosco Pound's books were translated and papers on his theories published, but major twentieth-century legal realist scholars were rarely introduced.

H.L.A. Hart's theory, which had been accepted since the late 1970s, was the starting point, and Lon Fuller and Ronald Dworkin's theories, which fueled debates with Hart, were largely accepted. Korean legal philosophers have actively researched them. These scholars hugely impacted Korean legal philosophy. Park indicates that under the influence of American jurisprudence, Korean legal philosophers have gradually expanded their scholarly interest beyond positive sources of law to the concrete processes of judicial decision-making. One of the most well-known salient features of the American tradition is the role of the court rather than the concept of law. Park describes Korean legal philosophers' critical attention to the court's interpretive activities.

Park proposes a future for Korean legal philosophy. First, while the study of legal philosophy's relationship to public law seems quite active, there has been insufficient research on its relationship to private law. Second, more attention should be paid to doing legal philosophy, which is more important for the study and teaching of legal philosophy. Third, the participatory quality of anti-positivist legal philosophy should be enhanced. Finally, the normative gaps between the positivist sources thesis and anti-positivist moral requirements should be considered the foundations of law.

Notes

1 Chongko Choi, *East Asian Jurisprudence* (Seoul: Seoul National University Press, 2009), 3–42.
2 William Twining, *General Jurisprudence: Understanding Law from a Global Perspective* (Cambridge: Cambridge University Press, 2009), 21.
3 Ibid.
4 H. L. A. Hart, *Essays in Jurisprudence and Philosophy* (Oxford: Oxford University Press, 1983), 88–89.
5 H. L. A. Hart, *The Concept of Law*, 2nd ed. (Oxford: Oxford University Press, 1994), 239–44.
6 William Twining, "General and Particular Jurisprudence: Three Chapters in a Story," in *Positivism Today,* ed. Stephen Guest (Aldershot: Dartmouth, 1996), 119–46.
7 Ronald Dworkin, *Law's Empire* (Cambridge: Harvard University Press, 1986), 90–96.
8 Twining, *General Jurisprudence*, 376–442.
9 Ibid., xi.
10 Ibid., 444–45.
11 For a brief overview of modern Korean history, see Young Woo Han, *A Review of Korean History Vol. 3: Modern/Contemporary Era*, trans. Chaibong Hahm (Paju: Kyongsaewon, 2010).
12 Chaihark Hahm and Sung Ho Kim, *Making We the People: Democratic Constitutional Founding in Postwar Japan and South Korea* (New York: Cambridge University Press, 2015), 166–67. Chaihark Hahm and Sung Ho Kim closely compare and analyze the process of constitutional enactment in Korea and Japan after 1945. They argue that the Founding Constitution of 1948 established the Republic of Korea by negation of the "double tyranny" of Japanese colonialism and pre-colonial monarchy (Hahm and Kim, 193).
13 For the discrepancy between the rule of law and the people's observation of the law during the 1960s, see Pyong-Choon Hahm, *The Korean Political Tradition and Law*, 2nd ed. (Seoul: Royal Asiatic Society, 1971), 187–204; Pyong-Choon Hahm and Seung-Doo Yang, "The Attitudes of the Korean People toward Law," *Yonsei Law Journal* 4, no. 2 (2013): 119–74 (originally written based on a 1962–1963 social scientific survey and republished in this journal).
14 According to Korean usage, the surname is written first, followed by the given name. Since it is common to use the Korean style in foreign broadcasts, the president's names will be written in the Korean style. But, for other people's names in this book, surnames will follow given names in the Western style.
15 Young Woo Han, *A Review of Korean History*, 214.
16 Ibid., 223.
17 For the political process leading to the creation of the 1987 Constitution, see James M. West and Edward J. Baker, "The 1987 Constitutional Reforms in South Korea: Electoral Processes and Judicial Independence," *Harvard Human*

Rights Yearbook 1 (1988): 135–77. For various papers on the legal system and legal phenomena in Korea, see a collection of articles by the late James M. West, *A Critical Discourse on Korean Law and Economy*, ed. Jae Won Kim (Seoul: Hanguel, 2002).

18 Dae-Kyu Yoon, ed., *Recent Transformations in Korean Law and Society* (Seoul: Seoul National University Press, 2000), 11–12.

19 Kun Yang, "The Constitutional Court and Democratization," in *Recent Transformations Law and Society*, ed. Dae-Kyu Yoon (Seoul: Seoul National University Press, 2000), 34–35.

20 Regarding the development of natural law theory in Korea, see Dokyun Kim, "Hanguk Pobchegyeeseo Jayeonpoblon-ui Hyeongseong-gwa Baljeon: Gwageoleul Doedolabomyeo Milaeleul Ganeumhanda [Formation and Development of Natural Law Theory in the Korean Legal System: Looking back on the Past and Prospecting for the Future]," in *Hanguk Hyeondae Beobcheolhag-ui Hyeongseong-gwa Jeongae [The Forming and Unfolding of Contemporary Legal Philosophy in Korea]*, ed. Korean Association of Legal Philosophy (Seoul: Sechang Publishing House, 2010), 157–201.

21 For cases where this law was applied during the war, see Myung-Lim Park, *The Requiem for Peace: A Critical-Constructive Reflection on the Korean War* (Paju: Nanam, 2005), 325–38.

22 In-Sup Han, "Hangukjeonjaeng-gwa Hyeongsabeob [The Conflict between Power Politics and Legality during Wartime: On the Collaboration Trials and Massacre of Civilians during the Korean War (1950–1953)]." *Seoul Law Journal* 41, no. 2 (2000): 135–79.

23 Dongwoon Shin, ed., *Yoo Byungjin Beoblyulnonjib: Jaepangwan-ui Gomin [Byungjin Yoo's Legal Essays: A Judge's Agony]* (Seoul: Beopmunsa, 2008), 152–53. This book was originally published in 1952, during the war, by Judge Byungjin Yoo and republished in 2008. Judge Yoo published it during the war to promote fair and just trials based on social realities and to oppose both the harsh punishment of those serving the enemy and the public demands for this punishment.

24 Shin, *Byungjin Yoo's Legal Essays*, 105–7.

25 In-Sup Han, ed., *Jeongui-ui Beob, Yansim-ui Beob, Ingwon-ui Beob [The Law of Justice, the Law of Conscience, the Law of Human Rights]* (Seoul: Pakyoungsa, 2004), 203.

26 Supreme Court 1985. 1. 29. Sentencing, 74Do3501 [Violation of Emergency Decree, Contempt of Court]. This is the Supreme Court's acquittal of Kang on the criminal charges.

27 Han, *The Law of Justice*, 237–40.

28 Ibid., 280–81.

29 Ibid., 281.

30 Un-Jong Pak and In-Sup Han, eds., *5.18, Beobjeog Chaegim-gwa Yeogsajeog Chaegim [5.18, Legal Responsibility and Historical Responsibility]* (Seoul: Ewha Womans University Press, 1995), 225–57.

31 Hun-sup Shim, "Beobcheolhag, Hyeogmyeong, Kudeta: Geomchal-ui 5.18 Bulgiso Cheobun-eul Gyegilo [Philosophy of Law, Revolution, Coup d'etat: In the Wake of the Prosecutor's 5.18 Non-Indictment]," in *5.18, Beobjeog Chaegim-gwa Yeogsajeog Chaegim [5.18, Legal Responsibility and Historical Responsibility]*, eds. Un-Jong Pak and In-Sup Han (Seoul: Ewha Womans University Press, 1995), 65.

32 Constitutional Court 1995.12.15. Sentencing, 95Hunma221 • 233 • 297 (Merge).

33 Seoul High Court 1996.12.16. Sentencing, 96No1892.

Bibliography

Choi, Chongko. *East Asian Jurisprudence*. Seoul: Seoul National University Press, 2009.

Dworkin, Ronald. *Law's Empire*. Cambridge: Harvard University Press, 1986.

Hahm, Chaihark, and Sung Ho Kim. *Making We the People: Democratic Constitutional Founding in Postwar Japan and South Korea*. New York: Cambridge University Press, 2015.

Hahm, Pyong-Choon. *The Korean Political Tradition and Law*. 2nd ed. Seoul: Royal Asiatic Society, 1971.

Hahm, Pyong-Choon, and Seung-Doo Yang. "The Attitudes of the Korean People toward Law." *Yonsei Law Journal* 4, no. 2 (2013): 119–74.

Han, In-Sup, ed. *Jeongui-ui Beob, Yangsim-ui Beob, Ingwon-ui Beob [The Law of Justice, the Law of Conscience, the Law of Human Rights]*. Seoul: Pakyoungsa, 2004.

Han, In-Sup. "Hangukjeonjaeng-gwa Hyeongsabeob [The Conflict between Power Politics and Legality during Wartime: On the Collaboration Trials and Massacre of Civilians during the Korean War, 1950–1953)]." *Seoul Law Journal* 41, no. 2 (2000): 135–79.

Han, Young Woo. *A Review of Korean History Vol. 3: Modern/Contemporary Era*. Translated by Chaibong Hahm. Paju: Kyongsaewon, 2010.

Hart, H. L. A. *Essays in Jurisprudence and Philosophy*. Oxford: Oxford University Press, 1983.

———. *The Concept of Law*. 2nd ed. Oxford: Oxford University Press, 1994.

Kim, Dokyun. "Hanguk Pobchegyeeseo Jayeonpoblon-ui Hyeongseong-gwa Baljeon: Gwageoleul Doedolabomyeo Milaeleul Ganeumhanda [An Investigation of the Formation and Development of Natural Law Theory in Modern Korea]." In *Hanguk Hyeondae Beobcheolhag-ui Hyeongseong-gwa Jeongae [The Forming and Unfolding of Contemporary Legal Philosophy in Korea]*, edited by Korean Association of Legal Philosophy, 157–210. Seoul: Sechang Publishing House, 2010.

Korean Association of Legal Philosophy, ed. *Hanguk Hyeondae Beobcheolhag-ui Hyeongseong-gwa Jeongae [The Forming and Unfolding of Contemporary Legal Philosophy in Korea]*. Seoul: Sechang Publishing House, 2010.

Lee, Chul-woo. "Democratization and Legal Change in South Korea: Overview." *The Review of Korean Studies* 6, no. 2 (2003): 3–26.

Pak, Un-Jong, and In-Sup Han, eds. *5.18, Beobjeog Chaegim-gwa Yeogsajeog Chaegim [5.18, Legal Responsibility and Historical Responsibility]*. Seoul: Ewha Womans University Press, 1995.

Park, Myung-Lim. *The Requiem for Peace: A Critical-Constructive Reflection on the Korean War*. Paju: Nanam, 2005.

Shim, Hun-sup. "Beobcheolhag, Hyeogmyeong, Kudeta: Geomchal-ui 5518 Bulgiso Cheobun-eul Gyegilo [Philosophy of Law, Revolution, Coup d'etat: In the Wake of the Prosecutor's 5.18 Non-indictment]." In *5.18 Beobjeog Chaegim-gwa Yeogsajeog Chaegim*, edited by Un-Jong Pak and In-Sup Han, 40–65. Seoul: Ewha Womans University Press, 1995.

Shin, Dongwoon, ed. *Yoo Byeongjin Beoblyulnonjib: Jaepangwan-ui Gomin [Byungjin Yoo's Legal Essays: A Judge's Agony]*. Seoul: Beopmunsa, 2008.

Twining, William. "General and Particular Jurisprudence: Three Chapters in a Story." In *Positivism Today*, edited by Stephen Guest, 119–46. Aldershot: Dartmouth, 1996.

———. *General Jurisprudence: Understanding Law from a Global Perspective*. Cambridge: Cambridge University Press, 2009.

West, James M. A. *Critical Discourse on Korean Law and Economy*. Edited by Jae Won Kim. Seoul: Hanguel, 2002.

West, James M. A., and Edward J. Baker. "The 1987 Constitutional Reforms in South Korea: Electoral Processes and Judicial Independence." *Harvard Human Rights Yearbook* 1 (1988): 135–77.

Yang, Kun. "The Constitutional Court and Democratization." In *Recent Transformations in Korean Law and Society*, edited by Dae-Kyu Yoon, 33–46. Seoul: Seoul National University Press, 2000.

Yoon, Dae-Kyu, ed. *Recent Transformations in Korean Law and Society*. Seoul: Seoul National University Press, 2000.

Constitutional Court 1995.12.15. Sentencing, 95Hunma221•233•297 (Merge).

Seoul High Court 1996.12.16. Sentencing, 96No1892.

Supreme Court 1985.1.29. Sentencing, 74Do3501 [Violation of Emergency Decree, Contempt of Court].

1 Legal Philosophy and Social Change in Korea

Dong-Ryong Shin and Jeong-Oh Kim

1 Introduction

It is said that the philosophy of law is 'the final and supreme court' of positive law, but legal philosophy and philosophers would face an enormous burden if required to answer all legal questions.[1] Instead, legal philosophy only allows us to think broadly, free from the prejudices and distortions of legal practice, analyze problems, and construct rational arguments leading to diverse and defensible conclusions.[2]

For these tasks, the philosophy of law must speculate on the social context and ideas of law. While legal ideas are generally considered universal and, thus, legal philosophy as a universal science, they must be understood within a particular time and place. Otherwise, research into legal ideas would be self-satisfying, unable to critique legal issues, and without innovative arguments. Legal philosophies from Western countries closely relate to their historical contexts. In the mid-twentieth century, natural law theory was revived to respond to positive law's failure to prevent Nazi atrocities. Comprehending critical legal studies' ascent in the 1980s requires understanding the 1960s–1970s political, social, and cultural climate in the West, especially the anti-war, counter-culture, and civil rights movements in the United States.

Korean legal philosophers have focused on liberation and modernization, liberty and equality, democracy, and the rule of law in their society. They explored but did not blindly accept Western legal philosophies, including natural law theory, legal positivism, liberalism, and communitarianism. Instead, these scholars selected theories appropriate to Korea's social context and developed an indigenous legal philosophy.

We examine the dialectical relationship between the universal and particular to trace the development of Korean legal philosophy. We divide this process into four periods: (1) liberation from Japanese imperialism and recovery from the Korean War (1945–1950s); (2) authoritarianism and the democracy movement (1960s–1980s); (3) the democracy movement's success and the transition to democracy (late 1980s–early 1990s); and (4) the expansion of liberalism and value pluralism (late 1990s–present).

DOI: 10.4324/9781003156437-2

2 Korean Legal Philosophy: Colonization, Liberation, and the Korean War

2.1 Liberation from Japanese Imperialism

During Japan's colonization of Korea (1910–1945), the colonial government established Kyung-sung Imperial University in Seoul and its law faculty, but Korean students were not interested in studying laws that the Japanese government enacted to govern Japan and its colonies. Japan's imperial Constitution enshrined the sovereignty of Tenno (Japanese emperor) and prescribed limited rights for the imperial Diet (parliament) and people. However, there were debates over whether this Constitution was enforceable in Korea. For example, the imperial parliament empowered the governor-general of Korea to make laws, which constrained Koreans' rights, raising questions about whether the governor's orders were constitutional. Several Japanese legal professors at Kyung-sung University argued that, although the imperial Constitution applied to Korea, separate governance was necessary to accommodate the country's distinctive language, customs, and systems. Other Japanese scholars insisted that the governor's orders were effective legislation in Korea, supplanting the Constitution. Still others contended that, based on Hans Kelsen's *Pure Theory of Law*, constitutional articles relating to governance applied in Korea, but civil rights provisions need not.[3]

Though Korean students were little interested in studying the positive law of Japan in this colonial situation, they had an opportunity to learn philosophy of law. Tomoo Otaka, a young Japanese professor at Kyung-sung University, began teaching 'law and philosophy' in the 1930s – the first legal philosophy course in Korea. Otaka was deeply immersed in Kant's critical philosophy, Husserl's phenomenology, and Kelsen's legal theory. Early in his teaching career, he treated Korean students as students, not colonized people, and freely interacted with them. Jin-Oh Yoo, Hang-Nyeong Yi, and San-Duk Hwang, who laid the foundation for Korean legal philosophy after liberation, attended Otaka's seminars and, under his guidance, began their studies. However, according to their memoirs, they sought to satisfy an intellectual thirst, not focus on the critical legal thinking involved in pursuing just laws.[4]

After the outbreak of the Sino-Japanese and Pacific wars, Otaka embraced imperialism and militarism. He argued that, because Japan warred for peace and development, colonial Korean students should become the emperor's people and accept Japan's 'great mission.' To discipline rebellious Korean students, Otaka argued that the 'Japanese spirit' should permeate the Korean Peninsula and its twenty-four million Koreans should become fully Japanese, making Korea a righteous nation.[5]

Otaka wrote *The National Structural Theory* (1936) and *The Essence of Law* (1942) based on the legal theories of Georg Jellinek, a famous public law scholar in Prussia. Otaka claimed that a political power within the positive law can make or destroy the law, but this power must obey a fundamental norm. Hesitating to label this norm natural law, Otaka termed it "the essence of law." Describing this essence as universal and particular for each country, he argued there is a universal democracy, but the Tenno system fits Japan. Korean students criticized him for turning into an imperialist and did not further participate in his classes.[6]

After liberation in 1945, Korean legal scholars began laying the groundwork for independent academic research, and they first needed to overcome Otaka's imperialist philosophy. They began translating Western scholarship, for example, Hans Kelsen's *Pure Theory of Law* (translated by San-Duk Hwang, 1949) and Gustav Radbruch's *Introduction of Legal Philosophy* (translated by Sung-Bae Kim, 1958). Other scholars introduced Roscoe Pound, Rudolf Stammler, Lon Fuller, and Eugen Ehrlich, among others. These activities provided an accurate understanding of the Western theories that Japanese legal scholars had distorted to serve imperialism. Colonial-era Japanese scholars, immersed in German legal positivism, had sought justifications for their country's totalitarian political system. They ignored the value-relative ideas of democracy presupposed in Kelsen's writings and understood his theory only as a part of a value-blind legal positivism. San-Duk Hwang, the first professor of legal philosophy at Seoul National University, contextualized his Korean translation of Kelsen's *Pure Theory of Law*.

> I don't want to call myself Kelsenian, but I believe that the independence of Korean jurisprudence can be realized only by overcoming Japanese jurisprudence. Considering that Japanese jurisprudence was influenced more by Kelsen than any other Western theorist, I took him as my starting point for legal research before moving beyond Kelsen.[7]

2.2 Judicial Practice During the Korean War

On June 25, 1950, the Korean War broke out and continued for three years, devastating South and North Korea and leaving indelible economic and social scars. During the first months, North Korean forces invaded the South and drove South Korean, US, and allied militaries operating under the UN banner to a small defensive area in the South (the Pusan Perimeter). UN forces counter-attacked and invaded the North; the North, with its Chinese allies, then pushed UN forces south. By the summer of 1951, a stalemate existed around the 38th parallel, which lasted until the July 1953 armistice ending military hostilities.

The South Korean government issued emergency decrees leading to the execution and other punishment of numerous innocent citizens. Several cases related to *The Special Ordinance for Measuring the Specified Crimes under the Emergency Period*, which became effective on June 25, 1950, the day the Korean War broke out. The ordinance sought to severely and promptly punish crimes against the country during a national emergency. Illegal conduct included active collaborations and passive assistance, such as providing information to or guiding northern forces. South Koreans often passively assisted to survive the North Korean occupation. Punishment ranged from more than ten years imprisonment to death.

The ordinance was procedurally deficient, permitting speedy-summary trials in a military court, lacking serious evidentiary standards, and denying appeals. Thousands of judicial killings were legalized and carried out. Because the Korean War was an extreme ideological conflict, opposing this law risked being labeled a communist North Korean sympathizer.[8]

Under these circumstances, Judge Byung-Jin Yoo first introduced natural law theory into Korean judicial practice. Applying *Zumutbarkeit* criminal legal theory, which supports punishment only if legal obedience can be expected, he saved many suspected collaborators. Yoo thought deeply about the ordinance's effectiveness, and, in articles published in 1952, he asked, "If observing the law leads to ignoring reality and following reality leads to violating the law, should we respect the law or the reality of social life?"[9] Advancing a natural law theory, he argued that judges must confront the law that ignores justice because legal norms that ignore social reality are evil, not justice.[10]

Imperial Japan's legal system, which insisted on ideologies representing the so-called Greater East Asia Co-Prosperity Sphere and Tenno sovereignty, did not recognize universal human rights. And it was difficult to assert a natural law theory under Japanese Imperialism. After liberation, Korean scholars could not actively pursue natural law theory because they lacked knowledge of diverse legal philosophies. Thus, Judge Yoo's writings were not based on a systematic natural law theory; but Korean jurists, for the first time, recognized that natural law was needed in their wartime context where a proper legal system was absent and unjust laws were enacted.

3 Korean Legal Philosophy During Authoritarianism

3.1 A History of Oppression and Resistance

3.1.1 Rhee's Authoritarianism and the April Revolution

The Korean War ended in 1953 with an armistice between South and North Korea, but the war's negative impact on Korean politics lasted. Most importantly, anti-communism became South Korea's official ideology and ushered in authoritarianism, which lasted until the civil democratic revolution in 1987.[11] Rhee Syngman, the republic's first president, trampled democratic aspirations to maintain his regime for twelve years (1948–1960). For example, in July 1959, he arrested and executed Jo Bong-Am, a strong competitor in the 1956 presidential election, on charges of state rebellion and communist espionage, and he disbanded the Progressive Party for the same reasons.[12] The Rhee government then rigged the March 15, 1960, presidential election, sparking a large-scale demonstration where students and other citizens demanded a new vote. Riot police responded, killing many. The April 20 "Declaration for Democracy of 300 Professors" decisively led to Rhee's April 26 resignation and US exile. This was the April Revolution.[13]

3.1.2 Park's Dictatorship and the Yushin Constitution

After the April Revolution, a democratic parliamentary cabinet was established in June 1960 according to the amended Constitution. However, eleven months later, in May 1961, military elites, led by Major General Park Chung-Hee, staged a coup d'état, beginning twenty-six years of a military dictatorship that lasted until 1987. Park was elected president three times in 1963, 1967, and 1971 through constitutional amendments, and he revised the Constitution in 1972 to take power permanently – the so-called Yushin (Revitalization) reform. A referendum approving the new Constitution occurred under martial law. An electoral college system – the National Conference for Unification – replaced direct presidential elections. The president had unlimited powers to appoint and dismiss the cabinet and prime minister and designate one-third of the National Assembly. Article 53 empowered the president to take emergency measures to temporarily suspend public freedoms and rights when he determined that national security or public safety and order were threatened. Park labeled the Yushin Constitution "Korean-style" democracy and justified it through alarmist claims of North Korean and internal communist threats.[14]

Many university students and civil rights activists struggled against the Yushin regime, leading Park to proclaim *Emergency Decrees No. 1* and *No. 2* prohibiting "any acts denying, opposing, distorting or slandering the Constitution of the Republic of Korea" and "any arguments, proposals or petitions for revising or abolishing the Constitution." Violators were tried in military courts and could be punished with up to fifteen years imprisonment plus fifteen years of suspended civil rights.[15] When the National League of Democratic Youth and Students (NLDYS) prepared a large-scale protest in 1974, Park issued *Emergency Decree No. 4*, which proclaimed:

> Those who have joined, financially supported, praised and encouraged the NLDYS, or met with its members, will be punished up to the death penalty. Regardless of involvement with the NLDYS, any student who conducted assemblies, protests, criticisms, or sit-ins, in or outside a school, will be punished up to the death penalty.[16]

The authorities insisted that the NLDYS was an illegal communist organization seeking to rebuild the People's Revolutionary Party that had attempted to overthrow the government with North Korean support.[17] The Supreme Court sentenced eight civil rights activists to death for violating *Emergency Decree No. 4*; the government executed the activists eighteen hours later.[18]

3.1.3 Chun's Military Coup and the 5.18 Gwangju Democratization Movement

Following these events, Jae-Gyu Kim, the Korean Central Intelligence Agency (KCIA) chief and Park's long-time right-hand man, assassinated Park on

October 26, 1979, abruptly ending the Yushin regime. The Korean people, expecting a restored democracy, demanded an early constitutional revision and parliamentary election. Unfortunately, history repeated in 1980. Chun Doo-Hwan, Roh Tae-Woo, and the newly emerging military elites mounted a military coup on December 12. They expanded martial law across the country, established an emergency governing organization, and dissolved the National Assembly. Protesters gathered in Seoul and other large cities, including violent protests in Gwangju from May 18–27. Chun responded to the Gwangju protests with military force,[19] killing and 'disappearing' at least 207 people, with 2,392 injured.[20] After the May 18 Gwangju Democratization Movement, pro-democracy demonstrations erupted across the country, but Chun was elected president through indirect elections.

3.2 A Dark Age for Natural Law Theory

After the Korean War, legal scholars founded the Korean Association of Legal Philosophy in 1957, but they were not passionate about the study of legal philosophy. It was more important for Korean legal scholars to analyze civil law, criminal law, and the other laws enacted by the country's first modern legislature. However, the 1960 April Revolution significantly impacted legal scholars, spurring them toward studying human rights, especially the right to resist in the Korean political context. Some focused on natural human rights, justifications for state power, and civil disobedience. Hang-Nyeong Yi, a Korea University professor, argued that the April Revolution was a triumph for natural law and justice.[21]

Although the Park-led coup negated the April Revolution, graduate students acquired a deep interest in natural law theory. Some students at West German universities obtained their doctoral degrees under the auspice of famous legal philosophers, who explored natural law theories from the perspective of substantial justice after World War II, including Erik Wolf, Hans Welzel, and Werner Maihofer. After returning to Korea, they were expected to contribute to Korean legal philosophy but could not actively publish.

One major reason for the publication reluctance seems to be the 1967 East Berlin-North Korean spy ring incident that was fabricated by the Park regime. The KCIA claimed that 194 Korean students and residents in West Germany and France visited North Korean embassies in East Berlin and Pyeongyang for espionage training and other anti-South Korean activities. The KCIA forcibly returned them to South Korea. Though no one was convicted of espionage during the final trial in the Supreme Court, legal philosophers studying in West Germany felt threatened,[22] hindering their research into natural law theory and substantial justice.

Park and Chun's regimes were also low points for the rule of law and democracy, and a deadly period for lawyers. The 5.18 Gwangju incident and the *Policy for Merger and Abolition of the Press* in 1980 were carried out by physical force, and it was even difficult for law professors to lecture on the idea of the rule of law.

Just as Nazism suppressed German philosophy of law, authoritarianism constricted Korean philosophy of law during the 1970s and 1980s.

During these dictatorships, research into legal philosophy was nothing more than theoretical and speculative studies on universal law and not based on Korea's reality. For example, some scholars studied Western natural law theories but did not place them in the Korean context. They failed to criticize judges' legal interpretations and applications, despite potential philosophical criticisms of many criminal cases. In the cases of the *People's Revolutionary Party* and *The National League of Democratic Youth and Students*, the death penalty could have been challenged based on Cesare Beccaria's *Crime and Punishment.* John Stuart Mill's *On Liberty* supported arguments that the *National Security Act*[23] unreasonably restricted freedom of thought and expression. However, Korean legal philosophers seemed like hermits, and academic articles were silent.

It is noteworthy that the theory of natural law was advocated by human rights activists, who were arrested for violating *Emergency Decrees No.1* and *No. 4* or the *National Security Act.* For them, natural law was not only an antithesis against so-called Korean-style democracy, but a thesis of resistance based on the universality of human rights. Thomas Aquinas' natural law theory played an especially important role, and Catholic priests, bishops, and cardinals attempted to protect students and other citizens in the democracy movement. Catholic Bishop Chi Hak-Soon, who was arrested for violating *Emergency Decree No.1* and *No. 4* in 1974, issued a statement (later known as "Cardinal Chi Hak-Soon's Proclamation of Conscience") condemning the Yushin Constitution as "a device abrogating citizens' inalienable human rights and human dignity by a single ruler with the help of an emergency decree" and declaring the Constitution "invalid as it was fabricated through violence, threat, and fraudulent referendum." He claimed that the emergency decrees were the most brutal destruction of natural law in Korean history.[24]

Unlike Judge Byung-Jin Yoo, judges during the Park regime rejected natural law arguments. The judiciary was, in fact, powerless because it was also subject to emergency decrees under Article 53 of the Yushin Constitution. While previous constitutions stipulated that judges rule according to "the Constitution," Article 101 of the Yushin Constitution required conformity with "this Constitution" and laws. Dokyun Kim has argued that this article made it difficult for judges to invoke universal civil rights and legal principles guaranteed by previous constitutions. Although judges may have felt a moral conflict, the new Constitution seemingly compelled convictions for most defendants accused of violating the emergency decrees.[25]

Unsurprisingly, the Supreme Court rejected the NLDYS' arguments based on natural law and the right of resistance in a 1975 case:

> The defendants, in this case, asserted that their acts were not illegal because they have a right of resistance. However, the concept of the right of resistance is very vague. This is a theory advocated by very few. The defendants' assertion

> is nothing more than a claim within the natural law, which ignores the existing positive law. They are only claiming the right of resistance to justify their illegal acts. The exercise of judicial power must be conducted within the positive law on the premise of the existing constitutional order. The judge's task is to maintain the state's legal order under these premises. For this reason, it is never acceptable that 'this judge' must accept their assertion.[26]

The Supreme Court's decision, embracing blind legal positivism, did not determine whether the emergency decrees were justified.

3.3 Blind or Critical Legal Positivism

During the 1960s and 1970s, scholar's legal research and judge's legal practice dealt mainly with legal positivism, like nineteenth-century Prussian jurisprudence, which had contributed to the widespread belief that even an 'evil law is law.' Since the 1980s, attempts to overcome value-blind legal positivism were led by Hun-Sup Shim, successor to San-Duk Hwang at Seoul National University. His research was based on analytical positivism, a philosophy not concerned with universal human rights, the right of resistance, or civil disobedience. His articles offered no critique of dictatorship in direct way. For this reason, a student opined,

> I started to feel dissatisfied with Professor Shim. Our legal reality was not contained in his books or papers. In the 1970s and 1980s, his writings did not mention the reality of the unjust, tyrannical political situation in our country where people were trampled by soldiers' shoes and tear gas (German cases were sometimes mentioned). In other words, his philosophy of law has always taken issue only with a universality that is valid anywhere and anytime. He could not escape the abstract ideal and contemplate our concrete reality.[27]

Understandably, a student who resisted the Korean dictatorship was not satisfied with Shim, but Shim's research cannot be seen as merely avoiding legal reality. His analytical legal positivism could be a passive critique of judicial practices that interpreted and applied the law through the logic of force rather than the logic of law. Moreover, Tae-Yeon Han, who argued a constitutional theory based on Carl Schmitt's natural rights, supported the Yushin Constitution, demonstrating that natural law theory, like blind legal positivism, can contribute to anti-democratic authoritarianism.[28] Paradoxically, analyzing the logic and meaning of universally valid laws regardless of reality could at least have led to supporting the formal rule of law. Shim presented his point of view in the translator's introduction to the *Anthology of Hans Kelsen's Legal Theory*:

> Jurisprudence is truly a 'practical science.' But now it is under the dark cloud of ideology. . . . It is taken for granted that an issue on 'post-ideology'

> itself is thought to be nonsense. In spite of Kelsen's declaration of inability, practical reason has been restored and has become a cornerstone of natural law. Justice, furthermore, is being projected vigorously despite Kelsen's demolition of idolatry. However, reading Kelsen's writings, we are acutely aware of how cold-hearted a legal scholar must be and how scientific or critical a legal philosopher must be. The value that a science pursues is truth. Even if its appearance sometimes makes you shudder, you have to look straight ahead. The task to realize truth in our reality is entrusted to practice and action. You can't do this in the name of science. If so, the truth will be perverted.[29]

Shim did not stop at Kelsen's legal theory. His thoughts advanced toward critical legal positivism to overcome the problem of blind legal positivism:

> In modern society, denying the positive law itself is like giving up our life. As such, positive law is inextricably linked with our life. In this respect, the contribution of legal positivism to our reality must be acknowledged. This insistence, however, should not be taken too far. It is clearly wrong to regard the legislator as an omnipotent being who can make law from anything and everything. We must overcome and rectify this error of legal positivism. . . . The legal order must be an order that guarantees human rights and peaceful order, which should be the minimum ensured by the positive law and the essence secured by legislators and executors. Our theory, on this basis, must advance toward realistic and healthy legal positivism, that is, critical legal positivism.[30]

From this standpoint, Shim wrote a series of papers implicitly criticizing Chun's regime without discussing the social-political reality. A representative article was the *Study on the Effectiveness of Law*, written in 1980 when Chun became president after suppressing the Gwangju democratization movement. Shim argued that power theory, which bases legal effectiveness on de facto power, is a nonsense that recognizes the rule of gangsters as the rule of law. Shim countered that the basis for the law's true normative effectiveness is not a tyrannical and arbitrary command, but a law-making authority approved by the public majority. Although a 'legal idea' cannot be easily defined, it must include justice, human dignity, liberty, equality, justification, and recognition of the majority of the people. Effective positive law contains an "existing 'Oughtness'" in which the legal idea is embodied. Shim concluded his paper: "There is no government that is not ultimately based on the will of the people, and there is no country where popular sovereignty is not a social fact."[31]

Dokyun Kim, Shim's successor at Seoul National University, recalled that many students concerned with legal reality were deeply impressed by this paper's implicit message and referred to Shim's thesis when questioning the effectiveness of current laws. Kim suggested that this reaction arose from many students becoming interested in legal philosophy in the early 1980s.[32]

3.4 What is a Korean Legal Culture?

In the 1970s and 1980s, some legal philosophers raised new issues regarding Korea's political and economic situation. Under the Yushin Constitution, authoritarian political leaders tried to promote modernization for economic development while emphasizing Korea's special situation. Korea's rapid economic development was labeled the 'Miracle of the Han River.' There was also a strong trend of defending Confucian community ethics and national identity against a liberal Western culture.

Contemporaneously, Korean legal philosophers recognized that the Western legal system did not fit traditional Korean culture and sought to combine the disparate systems. Their discourses revealed a tension between universality and particularity. This was not a conflict between democracy and anti-democracy but a gap between Korean traditions and the Western legal system. Korean leaders tried to accommodate the Western system for the economic and cultural modernization. However, the Western legal system and Korean traditional culture partially diverged because, while Westernized legal norms regulated economic life, Korean Confucian traditions dominated public behavior and conscious. Harmoniously combining those paradigms emerged as an important issue. There were several attempts to clarify the uniqueness of Korean traditional culture and suggest ways to reduce the divergence. Pyong-Choon Hahm and Hang-Nyeong Yi pioneered this research.

Hahm sought to discover the cultural logic inherent in Korean traditional culture. He received a J.D. from Harvard Law School in 1959 and was appointed as a professor in the law department at Yonsei University. While teaching philosophy of law, Hahm researched the legal consciousness of Koreans. He thought it important to understand Koreans' unique cultural logic to overcome transplantation hurdles. Analyzing the unique normative order and value system that governed Korean behavior, Hahm concluded that Korea is an affectional society, meaning Koreans believe that peace, harmony, and community solidarity outweigh truthfulness, justice, and individual liberty. Rather than relationships based on objective and rational judgments, they pursue affective relationships and aim for harmony and peace between the 'I' and the 'other.' Justice through legal judgments is rejected if it undermines harmony. Hahm explained,

> Law in Korea has been synonymous with punishment. Its foundation has been physical force. Law has been the antithesis of virtue, good, peace and harmony. It has been a detestable necessity at best and a symbol of violence, disruption, conflict, and bloodshed at worst. Order and peace have been based upon virtue and affection, never on punishment. The sword is the cause as much as the result of disorder and violence, and although it may be an indispensable equipment for the goddess of justice in the West, Koreans cannot help but feel an instinctive aversion to it. The sanguineness of the Western concept of justice prevents Koreans from accepting it wholeheartedly as the ideal of their social life.[33]

So, Koreans consider a litigious person a warlike one and litigation a threat to harmony and peace. If parties cannot achieve reconciliation through mediation and compromise, they are not acceptable members of the collectivity. Law then signifies the failure of princely virtue, and the administration of justice presupposes the breakdown of harmony and peace. Koreans have always favored mediators as peace-makers over judges, who lay down the law and affix blame.[34] Hahm insisted,

> The Rule of Law is a concept very dear to the hearts of lawyers in the West. It has become synonymous with the sum total of cherished Western political ideals. This concept has been transported to Korea as a part of the 'superior' civilization of the West, but it has been very slow in gaining ground there. The Korean linguistic equivalent of the concept means nothing more than rule by punishment. Such a concept has never been the ideal of the Korean people.[35]

Due to this alegalness of the Korean people, Hahm thought it unlikely Koreans would soon become a legal people. The traditional alegal way of life is inimical to the country's development and progress.[36] He maintained that, for Korea to modernize, it must not reject imported legal systems and revert to the normative customs of the living law. Although a perennial problem, the conflict between imported legal systems and the people's indigenous jural values should be at least minimized.[37]

3.5 Korean-Style Natural Law Theory: Pungto *Theory and* Gikbun *Ethics*

While Pyong-Choon Hahm presented Korean legal culture as distinct from its Western counterpart, Hang-Nyeong Yi went further, seeking to craft a distinct Korean legal conception based on East Asian legal thought. Insisting on natural law and the right to resist during the April Revolution, Yi sought to compose unique legal theories based on *gikbun* (職分) ethics.

Yi believed that, due to the typological relationship between humans and nature, history is neither universal nor particular but of a 'type,' which is a concept implying the particular while pursuing the universal. History is always a universally particular occurrence and a particularly universal occurrence. A historical type is created when universality gives the form and particularity provides the substance. Law ought to be understood in the context of historical types.[38] Typical laws, therefore, are "natural laws with variable contents." Natural law forms a legal idea, while positive law forms the legal reality.[39] Law's particularity and universality evolve and are completed by combining a natural law that transcends time and place with a positive law bounded by time and place.[40]

Importantly, such evolution presupposes *pungto* (風土) – a Korean word referring to a particular area's climate and environment, metaphorically expressing the society's tendencies, customs, institutions, and traditions. Yi regarded *pungto* as a material basis for normal living. Typifying laws as part of the *pungto* phenomenon, he argued that laws without *pungto* origins could not govern life, and laws that could not govern life would not be laws.[41] The laws of typified *pungto* are the natural laws that have gained concrete legitimacy for the people within the time and space of an era. In this reason, Yi's idea could be regarded as the theory of *pungtoic* natural law in a spatial sense, of historical natural law in a temporal sense, and of cultural natural law in a cultural philosophical sense.[42]

Yi sought to integrate dialectically the universality of human rights and the particularity of Korean society, thus revealing Korean law's *pungto* in history. He developed *gikbun* ethics – a Korean word referring to a role or duty related to one's occupation or social position. *Gikbun* is a moral concept originally used in the East and West during the ancient and medieval times. Yi argued that emphasizing *gikbun* ethics is not retreating to the medieval times but promoting modern contractual relationships. Contrary to the general idea that rights are benefits and duties are losses, rights and duties coexist within *gikbun*.[43]

Article 30 of the current Korean Constitution states: "(1) All citizens shall have the right to work. (2) All citizens shall have the duty to work. The State shall prescribe by Act the extent and conditions of the duty to work in conformity with democratic principles" (Enforcement date October 27, 1980). Yi claimed that this was a new idea that could change society from a competitive one, where rights and duties are considered oppositional, to a cooperative one, where they are complementary. There are duties in rights and rights in duties,[44] and this concept should be at the center of a new employee-employer relationship.

> It is most significant for human beings to maintain human dignity, and this human dignity is realized when they faithfully fulfill their *gikbun*. In contractual relations, the employer wants to profit at the worker's expense, and the worker wants to profit from the employer's loss. However, in *gikbun* ethics, it is a relationship of common interest. The employer's interests become the worker's interests, and the worker's interests become the employer's. A company should be a cradle and community where employers and workers can survive, be rewarded for creative acts, and enjoy their lives. The company is the foundation for all living and happiness that transcends employers and workers. Thus, the company's maintenance must take precedence over the interests of employers and workers.[45]

Gikbun ethics are an inherent part of the essence of a professional role and a citizen's duty. They shape the ethics of lawyers, medical doctors, journalists, and broadcasters, as well as political and environmental ethics. Yi considered *gikbun* ethics living norms and particular instances of natural law taking precedence over legal norms. He, thus, sought a Korean-style natural law rather than the West's universal natural law, and he tried to construct the foundation of Korea's positive law through g*ikbun* ethics.

However, Yi's theory is questionable. His *gikbun* ethics concerning a new worker-employer relationship may have been unrealistic considering that, when he proposed it, most laborers were barely guaranteed worker rights, did not receive a minimum wage, and lived poorly. Since the 1990s, his successor, Zai-Woo Shim, has overcome those limitations by placing universality above particularity.

4 Korean Legal Philosophy During Civil Revolution

4.1 Longing for Democracy

4.1.1 The New Resistance Movement

The oppressive social and political situation of the 1980s ironically gave some law students a strong motivation to study legal philosophy, and they often chose philosophy of law or sociology of law courses to overcome the legal nihilism. Jeong-Oh Kim recalled his agony:

> In our society, freedoms of speech, publication, assembly, and association guaranteed by the Constitution were suppressed to a tremendous extent. In such a situation, what I expected from a constitutional lecture was a constitutional critique of the distorted political and social situation. However, what I saw in lectures was a reconstruction of the grim situation. The professor's lecture explaining the theory of human rights was painful. I was so disappointed with jurisprudence's handmaid status that I had no academic interest in law. . . . After entering graduate school, I went on a wandering path to find an exit from the distorted legal knowledge and legal intellectuals in the philosophy of law.[46]

This new generation studied theories to resist the authoritarian regime. Thus, these students differed from those who majored in legal philosophy during the Japanese colonial period. Colonial-era legal philosophy was the antitheses of reality, and Otaka's disciples studied it mainly for intellectual curiosity. They also diverged from legal scholars in the 1970s, who were like hermits.

Although some students limited their contribution to intellectual criticism, others directly participated in the democracy and labor movements, and they sought ideological weapons against the dictatorship. This transformation was deeply related to the student-led democratization movement becoming more organized and energetic after the 5.18 Gwangju Uprising. Upon receiving a doctorate in philosophy of law or sociology of law at home or abroad, and after appointment as a university professor, they infused Korean legal philosophy with spirited critical voices. This phenomenon was similar to the critical legal studies movement launched by tenured law school professors in the United States, who had experienced the civil rights and anti-war movements in the 1960s and 1970s. It resembled the situation in West Germany and France, where the students who participated in the 1968 Revolution became critical or postmodern theorists.

4.1.2 The Civil Revolution of 1987

Korea's democratic revolution succeeded in 1987. The new Constitution adopted the direct presidential system, more strongly guaranteed public rights, expanded parliamentary powers, and introduced the Constitutional Court to determine a law's constitutionality. Although Roh Tae-Woo, the new military's second-in-command, was elected president after Chun Doo-Hwan, he was followed by Kim Young-Sam and then Kim Dae-Jung, democracy activists during the Park Chung-Hee regime. Just as the Korean economy developed quickly during and after the 1970s, Korean democracy has rapidly developed since 1987. President Kim Dae-Jung, a Nobel Peace Prize laureate, also laid the foundation for inter-Korean peace through a summit in 2000 with North Korean leader, Kim Jeong-Il – the first such meeting since the armistice. Anti-communist ideology no longer overpowered South Korea's aspirations for democracy and justice.[47]

The 1980s democracy movement contributed to a changing Korean legal philosophy, and, by 1987, the transformation was obvious. It was initiated by natural law theorists, who had been reclusive but were well-prepared to convince Koreans, once forced to accept that an 'evil law is also law,' that an 'evil law cannot be law.'[48] The young scholars lit intellectual torches by dedicating their lives to a legal philosophy or legal sociology resisting authoritarian regimes. Their legal philosophy sought to restore human dignity and democracy, abolish 'evil' laws, and punish dictators.

4.2 For Human Dignity and Democracy

Natural law theory was vigorously argued around 1987 and, unlike before, actively promoted by legal scholars. Their articles were not merely academic but aimed to reflect on and reform Korea's concrete legal reality. They prioritized universal human rights and democracy rather than Korean-style democracy. Zai-Woo Shim's theory of natural law is the most representative example.

Submitting his master's thesis on "A Study on the Foundation of Law's Effects" under Hang-Nyeong Yi in 1961, Shim obtained a Juris Doctor in 1973, writing on the "Right of Resistance and Human Dignity," under the auspice of Werner Maihofer at Germany's University of Bielefeld. His thesis insisted that a legal order's purpose must protect and guarantee human dignity, and the state ought to exist for humans according to the rule of law and constitutionalism.

However, after returning to Korea and publishing "Human Dignity and Legal Order: Especially Focusing on Kant's Idea of Order" in 1974, he did not produce articles on the right of resistance for thirteen years. During this period, he taught criminal law and studied East Asian legal philosophy. After 1986, he returned to publishing legal philosophy, writing on the abolition of torture and the importance of human dignity. He translated Werner Maihofer's *Rechtsstaat und Menschliche Wuerde* (*Rule of Law & Human Dignity*)[49] and Hela Mant's *Tyannislehre und Widerstandsrecht* (*Theory of Tyranny and the Right to Resistance*).[50] Shim's work insisted,

> We have lived only in a power state, and we have had little experience with a state where the rule of law is respected. During the authoritarian Joseon dynasty for five hundred years, Japanese militarism for thirty-six years, and Korean military authoritarianism for thirty years, we have hardly escaped state oppression. For a long time, we have been treated as mere means for political and national ends by the state power, and we have never been respected as an end. Our history has been nothing more than the history of an inhuman state. As a result, we have been living in a history where human enlightenment has stopped. It is time to ask seriously what the state means for humans – whether humans exist for the state or the state exists for humans.[51]

It is noteworthy that Shim not only claimed human dignity based on Western legal philosophy, but he constructed the foundations of human rights through East Asian philosophical traditions. He acknowledged Hang-Nyeong Yi's *gikbun* ethics but tried to solve the problem of universality and particularity by prioritizing human rights over Korean traditional norms.

Shim took a deep interest in East Asian legal philosophy and sought general principles and standards to justify the state and its laws.[52] He was convinced that there were normative principles inherent in living relationships and those principles were universally applicable in the West and East. However, he did not argue that a universal natural law guarantees human dignity worldwide. Rather, he emphasized a suitable and proper order in any concrete situation where humans enter into relationships. The order inherent in these living relationships is rooted in social facts.[53]

Shim argued that Confucius taught more than two millennia ago that an ethical social order arises only when people occupying different roles, such as the king and vassals, fulfill all obligations implied in their titles and official names. The Confucian concept, *myeong* (名), refers to the social title or role one bears, accompanied by *bun* (分), referring to one's share of duties. *Myeongbun* (*Mingfên*, 名分), which is still often invoked in East Asian societies to justify actions for a cause, means fulfilling one's role as a specific social being. Shim explained that the Confucian concept of rites (*li*, 禮) is the objectification of such justifiable causes as a code of behavior. The Western equivalent of rites is the law. Positive laws that concretize the notions of rites presuppose the presence of natural law as the source of their justification. According to Shim, the Confucian school labels this background natural law 'the way of things' (*dào lǐ*, 道理) or the 'internal logic of things' (*shìlǐ*, 事理). Similar to a concept of the nature of things, it refers to the individual principle inherent in beings and shapes, and it binds the substances of positive laws. It exactly matches the concept of concrete natural law or the systematic natural law mentioned in Maihofer's legal ontology.[54]

Shim insisted that the way of things, internal logic of things, or nature of things, referring to the specific principle inherent in being, still requires a more general principle to bind its specificity. The nature of things suggests the right law for each specific being, but it is not a perfectly just or legitimate law to govern all human society. It ought to presuppose a more general principle of order inherent in human relationships, but Shim thought that this problem could not be solved without returning to the idea of dignity. The concrete and historical natural law found in the nature of things forms a complete and justifiable legal order only through a dialectical relationship with a universal natural law that enshrines the dignity and personality of human beings as autonomous subjects. With an emphasis on universal human dignity, he tried to lessen the tension between universality and particularity.[55]

4.3 Abolishing Evil Laws

After the 1987 civil revolution, Korean legal scholars strongly criticized authoritarian laws suppressing democracy. Legal philosophers, especially young scholars in the 1980s, played an important role in this critical movement. Both moderate liberals and radical leftists were more interested in the practical sociology of law than the philosophy of law.

In 1987, twenty professors and graduate students organized the Korean Law & Society Association (KLSA). After two years of internal seminars on legal sociology, they held their first public conference in March 1989 on the "Public Debate for the Revision and Abolition of Anti-Democratic Evil Laws." Topics included a "Critique of the Revised Assembly and Demonstration Act," "The Issue of Revision and Abolition of the National Security Act," and a "Critique of the Social Safety Act and Security Observation Act." The conference attracted much public attention. Rather than abstract legal ideas, the KLSA focused on analysis and criticism of positive law to address the urgent need for concrete criticism of contemporary 'evil' laws. The association also dealt with South-North Korea unification, a controversial issue in Korea that was not freely debated due to the authoritarian regimes' anti-communist ideology.

Noteworthy was Kun Yang's paper, "The Law and Social Studies in Korea: Beyond Hahm's Theses." His several criticisms of Pyong-Choon Hahm's thesis provoked a controversy over the legal culture. He argued that Hahm's basic perspective on law and society was too narrowly confined to a culture-centric view. Although legal culture, including social attitudes and evaluations about the law, has a vital role in influencing a legal system's structure and substance, Hahm chiefly considered cultural elements among various factors affecting the legal system's function. Hahm excluded important non-cultural factors, such as the politico-social hierarchy.[56]

Yang asserted that it seemed superficial to conclude that the non-litigious attitudes of contemporary Koreans mainly result from a traditional preference for non-legal settlements. He instead suggested that lawsuit avoidance may have resulted from factors such as strong distrust of the judiciary under the authoritarian Park regime during the 1960s and 1970s, an extreme maldistribution of income during the period of rapid economic growth, which championed 'growth-first, distribution later,' and extremely high legal fees charged by the small lawyer monopoly existing when Hahm initiated his investigation.[57] Instead of Joseon Confucian ethics, Yang emphasized Koreans' avoidance of lawsuits during Japanese colonialism, which exerted more influence on Korean legal development.

> To make the matter worse, even after the First Republic of Korea was established in 1948, the colonial legal system under the Japanese rule was maintained in considerable parts[,] including the Criminal Code and the Civil Code[,] for a fairly long time until the late 1950's when new laws were promulgated. Still today, the real circumstances are that vestiges of repressive laws under the Japanese imperialism remain alive in some respects, particularly in the area of laws of politico-social control. For example, some remarkable resemblance can be seen between the Law for the Maintenance of Public Order under the Japanese rule and the National Security Act of today. Thus, the elements of [the] colonial, repressive legal system have not been eliminated through the successive authoritarian [regimes] since 1948. Along with that[,] the citizen's attitudes of distrust or avoidance toward law [have] gradually deepened.[58]

Yang's argument closely relates to his aspiration for liberal democracy. In his view, the deep-rooted evils of authoritarian regimes that followed Japanese imperialism would not be revealed if only cultural factors were thought to cause Korea's failed rule of law. The pro-Japanese authoritarian political and social system must be reformed to realize the rule of law. Since the 1990s, the KLSA, including Yang, has advocated abolishing anti-democratic laws and reforming the authoritative judicial system.

4.4 Revealing Capitalist Ideology

In 1989, several professors and graduate students complained that the KLSA was a critical anarchism at most. They withdrew and founded a new organization, the Democratic Legal Studies Association (DELSA). While the KLSA operated within democratic liberalism, the new association took a radical leftist position. To oppose positive laws exploiting the workers and people, they applied Marxist legal theory to analyze the Korean legal system. The founding declaration insisted that a new colonial fascist regime governed Korea, oppressing workers through fascist laws, bourgeois laws, and capitalistic legal ideologies.[59] They evaluated Korean laws as follows:

> The civil law, commercial law, and economic law ensure that the monopoly capitalists can appropriate and reproduce the means of production. The administrative law organizes the fascist system and facilitates its operation. The Constitution ideologically justifies and reproduces these laws in the name of 'liberal democracy.' In this way, all laws in South Korea are tools of the South Korean bourgeoisie to maintain the new colonial fascist system and suppress the national democratic movement of the working people.

> And the ideology of law, represented by the slogans of 'Rule of Law' and '*Rechtsstaat*,' conceals the ruling class' unjust acts and renders the ruled class faithful to the positive laws.[60]

Furthermore, they argued that natural law theory and legal positivism concealed class conflicts behind the positive law. Even if historically significant, natural law theory reflects only the ideology of bourgeois capitalism. The conceptual jurisprudence is pro-capitalist because it lacks awareness of class struggle and social conflicts.[61]

However, the 1990s downfall of socialist countries, such as East Germany and the USSR, undermined their arguments; so they reinterpreted theories of base-superstructure, the law's relative autonomy, and the withering of law. For example, they argued that the theory of legal withering does not seek to eliminate the law but to realize the people's participation in the legislative and law-enforcement processes by strengthening their autonomy and control over the legal system, which is inevitably coercive and oppressive. If we can enlighten people's norm-consciousness, they can create democratic and revolutionary laws to replace capitalist ones.[62]

Nevertheless, after the mid-1990s, the context for their research changed. Socialism failed, workers' rights were becoming institutionalized in Korea, and various social problems arose. Those were difficult to interpret through socialist legal theory. DELSA members tried to continue their mission toward liberation by moving beyond Marxist legal theory and turning to John Rawls' justice theory, German critical theory, postmodern legal theory, and American critical legal studies.

4.5 Punishing Dictators

Since 1988, political and legal measures have been implemented to eliminate the authoritarian regime's anti-democratic laws and other apparatuses. The National Assembly held hearings on the corruption of the Chun Doo-Hwan regime and the Gwangju massacre and organized the Committee on Revision and Abolition of the Anti-Democratic Law. The Constitutional Court significantly contributed to revising the *Social Protection Act*, *National Security Act*, and *Assembly and Demonstration Acts* and to abolishing the *Social Security Act* – all enacted by the military junta's emergency legislative body in 1980.[63]

During the civilian government of President Kim Young-Sam in 1995, the hottest legal issue was whether former presidents Chun Doo-Hwan and Roh Tae-Woo could be punished for the December 12, 1979, military coup and May 18, 1980, Gwangju massacre. On May 13, 1994, victims of the military junta's violent suppression of the Gwangju Democratization Movement filed a case against twenty-four major junta figures, including Chun and Roh, for insurrection, murder for the purpose of insurrection, mutiny, and related crimes. The Seoul District Public Prosecutor's Office decided not to prosecute the case, arguing that if after a coup a new constitution is enacted by a referendum and a new government established through a presidential election, the successful coup is not an insurrection, but a legitimate act publicly recognized as the new constitutional order. The prosecutor gave three legal philosophical grounds.[64]

First, according to German constitutional scholar Georg Jellinek, we must acknowledge that the new regime was established and recognize the normative power of the regime's *de facto* actions (an argument for normative power of the factual). Second, according to Hans Kelsen, if a political regime is successfully transformed, the new order becomes an effective legal order because the 'basic norm (*Grundnorm*)' has changed, and the new government has the power to make laws. If the transformation fails, the new order is ineffective, and its unsuccessful actions are criminally punishable because the new constitution is not enacted (argument for the transformation of the basic norm). Third, per Gustav Radbruch, when the old legal order is broken and a new one established, this transformation becomes the basis for the law, and the new law's effectiveness must be recognized for legal stability (argument for legal stability).

Korean legal philosophers, who were perplexed and displeased with the public prosecutor's philosophical arguments, immediately responded. Hun-Sup Shim, who advocated critical legal positivism, persuasively challenged the prosecutors' distorted arguments. Regarding Jellinek, Shim asserted that, although the military had received a political judgment, this was far from the certainty Jellinek envisioned. Shim argued that Jellinek endorsed a minimum ethics requirement for the law, and without this ethical foundation the law could be easily overthrown. His normative power of the factual could be recognized only if the law was supported by the conviction that it is as it should be. This conviction is the public's prevailing ethical belief based on justice and reason – the natural law element.[65] After a detailed analysis of the prosecutor's distortions of Kelsen and Radbruch, Shim concluded:

> For a law to be an effective norm, its feasibility should be largely guaranteed by organized coercion; its enactment and application must be based on authorization by a higher norm; and its binding power must presuppose the confidence of the majority of the people in this justification. For this reason, a successful coup d'état only achieves feasibility but does not gain public approval for its justification.[66]

Shim's argument was reflected in the "Opinion of Professors in the College of Law on the Constitutional Complaint related to the May 18 Gwangju Massacre." They asserted that the prosecutor's version of legal positivism could be supported only by the power theory, which would bury justice within the realm of power and had no justification.[67]

The Constitutional Court accepted Shim's view and clarified that the decision not to prosecute was unconstitutional. The Court held,

> The constitutional order, which is the legal interest protected by the *Criminal Act*'s punishment for insurrection, is based on the people's sovereignty and the basic order of a free democracy, not on the incumbent's power

> or the constitutional order maintained by such power. Even if a successful coup makes it practically impossible to punish the perpetrators during their incumbency, they can be punished whenever the constitutional institutions recover their proper function and thereby regain the power to punish the offenders.[68]

The justices further held,

> The amendment to the Constitution of the Fifth Republic was passed through a referendum, and the suspect, Chun Doo-Hwan, was elected president through an indirect election. Although these acts were formally in accordance with the provisions of the Constitution and laws of that time, they were done in a coercive atmosphere under martial law, and the truth was concealed. Also, they were performed by a representative institution that could not accurately reflect the will of the people. Therefore, it cannot be said that the insurrection was approved because the people freely decided their sovereign will. . . . The prosecutor's decision not to prosecute, on the grounds that a successful coup is immunized, is a misunderstanding of the Constitution's ideals and the criminal jurisprudence regarding insurrection and, therefore, is unlawful.[69]

While the Constitutional Court accepted a critical legal positivist argument, natural law arguments were reflected in the judgment of the court of appeals in charge of Chun and Roh's criminal punishment. After clarifying that the *de facto* impunity of the coup actors was neither recognition of the people's will nor immunity from criminality, the court commented,

> Since the Constitution is the supreme norm in the legal system, all laws can acquire legitimacy only when consistent with the Constitution. However, since legitimacy does not mean justification, a positive law with legitimacy does not necessarily mean a norm with justification. If there was a universal principle of law that contains the principles of justice, goodness, and peace, and, if it could be called natural law, only the constitution and laws that conform to these natural laws could be justified. Natural law is immutable, but its perception depends on the degree of enlightenment produced by human reason. If there is a widespread view in society that a constitution or basic legal order is unjust because it conflicts with natural law, and there is a clear struggle to overcome the injustice by force, we call it a revolution.[70]

Dokyun Kim concluded that this court decision was the Korean judiciary's first acceptance of natural law theory. Based on traditional Aquinas' natural law theory, the appeals court ruled that the purpose of a good government is not to suppress and infringe the public's rights, but to realize the safety and welfare of the people.[71]

5 Korean Legal Philosophy in the Age of Liberalism and Value Pluralism

5.1 New Missions

From 1987 to the mid-1990s, legal philosophers in Korea contributed faithfully to democratization, but their works had some problems. First, their intense criticism broke the cooperative relationship between legal practice and legal philosophy. They saw that the current legal practice could not recognize and enforce just laws, so they regarded themselves as the ultimate judges of existing legal practice and the experts providing reasonable solutions to legal authorities. This was a great burden. Above all, these scholars had poor theoretical tools to analyze Korea's legal reality and suggest alternatives. They had a strong tendency to introduce foreign theories widely accepted in the history of legal philosophy, and most of their papers were on Western legal philosophers. They thought that, if foreign legal theories were evaluated as universally valid, they would be valid for Korea's legal reality. Consequently, these scholars presented the philosophy of law as a universal science and the concept of universal human rights as suitable for the democratic movement. However, the more they relied on the terms and logic of Western legal philosophers, the more their legal philosophy discourse became distant from judicial practice.

The second problem was that, until the early 1990s, Korean philosophers' legal theories offered limited answers to new social issues. After the successful civil revolution, Korea rapidly transformed into a liberal society. Political democratization was achieved to some extent, and many efforts sought to realize political, economic, and social rights. Contemporaneously, problems associated with growing individualism increased sharply, with many groups claiming interests as rights. Various social issues surfaced, for example: NIMBY (not in my backyard), extreme regional conflicts, feminism, rights related to biotechnology and cyberspace, and political nihilism. However, traditional natural law theory and legal positivism had difficulties suggesting solutions to new social issues unrelated to democratization.

Korean legal philosophy needed a revised theoretical foundation, which the Korean Association of Legal Philosophy (KALP) offered. Since the mid-1990s, KALP, founded in 1957, has rapidly developed in quantity and quality. Around 1990, most of KALP's young scholars, who chose philosophy of law as their major in the 1980s, received doctoral degrees in Korea, Germany, and the United States. They work with various modern legal theorists, such as H.L.A. Hart, Ronald Dworkin, Joseph Raz, Robert Alexy, Jürgen Habermas, Niklas Luhman, Michel Foucault, Jacques Derrida and with philosophers from American Legal Realism, critical legal studies, and feminist legal theory. Most were appointed university professors, who taught in many disciples, including those who became law school professors around 2010. Their vigorous and various activities addressed new social issues and legal practices. Since the late 1990s, the main topics of Korean legal philosophy have been (1) the stable institutionalization of civil democracy; (2) Korea's new litigation culture; (3) a justice theory for a society with conflicting rights; (4) critiquing authoritative judicial practice through theories of legal reasoning; and (5) applying legal philosophy to new social issues. This new generation of scholars has tried to overcome the historical limitations of Korean legal philosophy.

5.2 Institutionalizing Civil Democracy

5.2.1 The Convergence of Legal Positivism and Natural Law Theory

Since the late 1990s, the public sphere of Korean society has democratically developed. The Constitutional Court has strived to realize the human rights guaranteed by the Constitution of 1987. Civil society criticized political and economic authoritarianism through rational discourse and actively participated in the legislative process. In this context, Korean legal philosophers have accepted new tasks to transform authoritarian legal positivism into a democratic legal positivism that could respect democratic legitimacy and transform the natural law's excessively moralistic and elitist theory into a democratic theory of natural law that recognizes the necessity of positive law.

Korean legal philosophers, who call themselves legal positivists, do not regard the law as the sovereign's command requiring the public's habitual obedience. Instead, they have been deeply interested in Hart's legal positivism since the late 1990s.[72] Above all, they consider Hart's legal system theory an important basis for constructing democratic legal positivism because it presupposes a 'rule of recognition' based on the people's critical and reflective attitudes. Nevertheless, they have cautiously accepted Hart's theory. They acknowledge like Hart that judges can exercise discretion to decide hard cases based on policy arguments. However, these philosophers question whether Korean judges can realize utilitarian solutions by employing policy discretion. This concern seems to have resulted from unconstitutional judicial decisions rendered according to the demands of authoritarian regimes. Korean legal philosophers are also reluctant to follow Joseph Raz's exclusive legal positivism because they do not trust that the legislature properly reflects the people's will. They are, instead, mainly focused on moral inclusive legal positivism, which accepts a minimal natural law content.[73]

However, this emphasis on a minimal natural law content may be a threshold for deviating from Hart's rule of recognition. Dokyun Kim attempted to cross that threshold. He understood that the moral norm included in Hart's rule of recognition is not an outcome of ex-post approval, but a conceptually inevitable thing already embedded in positive law. In Korea's Constitution, for example, the political principles of liberal democracy are adopted as basic principles. When understanding positive law according to this rule of recognition, Kim argued that Gustav Radbruch's thesis that an "Extremely Unjust Rule is not a Law" could be accepted and we should optimize the political principle of morality in hard cases.[74]

Thus, legal positivism and natural law theory have converged in Korean legal philosophy since the late 1990s. Natural law theorists in Korea fully agreed with the legal positivist's view, which understands the law as a social product constructed and formed only through public discussion. They were wary of excessive moralization of the law and sought to prevent an anti-democratic natural law theory, where a minority of elites tried to restrict the citizens' rights under the pretext of natural law. Consequently, they have argued for a weak natural law theory that considers reflective adjudication of the constitutionality of statutes as the key to realizing democracy in light of natural law.[75]

5.2.2 Institutional Natural Law Theory

Byung-Sun Oh, who obtained a Ph.D. under Neil MacCormick at the University of Edinburgh in 1991, believed that each institution consists of ideals, norms, and factual practices. He understood the institutional character of law in two ways: (1) as a clear expression of substantive norms confirmed by people's compliance with them and (2) as an implicit realization of the ideals and values governing the society. As the normative systems governing societies, modern constitutions simultaneously confirm the factual existence of positive norms and embody institutional moralities. Oh argued that Korea's 1987 Constitution is institutional natural law because it realizes institutional morality and governing ideals as the country's foundational principles.[76]

Oh proposed that institutional natural law theory favors an integrative approach to legal interpretation and a hermeneutical approach to constitutional interpretation. Integrative hermeneutics acknowledges the law's dual structure as comprising reason and command, and adopts analytical, historical, and teleological approaches to solve legal problems. A constitutional adjudication must conform to the positive legal rules and satisfy the rational requirements of the particular institutional morality. Since the constitution as an institution and constitutional morality as governing ideals seek to promote justice and the common good within a state, constitutional adjudication must produce the best and most rational outcome possible.[77]

5.2.3 Anthropological Natural Law Theory

As democratization has progressed, Korean natural law theorists have tried to expand natural law's application to various modern problems, not just those in the political field. Un-Jong Pak is representative of this group. After receiving a Dr. iur. from Germany's University of Freiburg in 1979, she was appointed as a professor at Ewha Womans University in 1980. Pak interpreted and criticized legal positivism using an anthropological theory of justice.

> The anthropological aspect of natural law can only be understood when it passes rigorous academic inspection of what human beings are. At this time, natural law theory contains human beings. The great achievement of the

> Western natural law theory is that it brought the ethical and existential horizons of human beings into legal thinking. . . . In order to recover true practical reason, we must break all stupid and wrong human relationships that do not fit our humanity. . . . Our mission is metaphysical if we understand the restoration of practical reason as building a bridge between science and *Existence*.[78]

She asserted that, if the legal idea is a value the law must realize, it must meet the standards of human beings. Of course, we cannot deny needing to understand the law as a rational objective rule and investigate it scientifically, but excessive rule-rationalism can render the law a thing superimposed on human *Existence*. Legal and theoretical radicalization carries this risk. Thus, Pak opposed any form of radical legal theory, such as Kelsen's *Pure Theory of Law*, which embraces extreme legalism by insisting on scientific jurisprudence, and Luhmann's legal functionalism, which deconstructs human autonomy into system's autonomy. She considered her position a passive theory of natural law, entailing minimal anthropology,[79] and she understood natural law theory as a critique of law, not as a moral theory.

> I think that this kind of lubricant for legal thinking is always necessary to expand the horizon of a judge's legal consciousness. Natural law theory is the result of the idea that the fundamental order of political and social communities cannot be left to arbitrary order. Since the laws and systems in reality are not perfect, the efforts toward a better system will continue. . . . In the end, the natural law is an ideology in which the law modifies itself. Self-correction idea does not need to be thought of as a unique product of Western culture. A community that distinguishes 'just law' from 'positive law' accepts this self-correction ideology of law.[80]

Pak studied various legal and philosophical themes from this standpoint, such as the anthropological basis of justice, legal and bioethics, technology and human rights, the rule of law and civil disobedience, feminist legal philosophy, and judicial reform. In her articles, she warned that what seems like humanity's advancement could paradoxically lead to domination over human beings.[81]

5.3 A Litigation Society

In the late 1990s, Korean legal philosophers faced a new legal reality where Koreans actively pursued their rights claims. Pyong-Choon Hahm argued that Koreans rarely used the official legal system because they highly value affective and alegalistic relationships. Contrary to his thesis, civil litigation has radically increased since the 1980s. Jeong-Oh Kim and Dohyun Kim empirically revealed Korean society's transformation into a litigation society.[82]

After reviewing civil litigation from 1953 to 2003, Dohyun Kim found a dramatic increase during the last twenty-five years of his study. From thirty thousand cases in 1960, civil filings rose to more than one million in 2002. An upward climb that began in 1980 has increasingly accelerated. The slope of the curve in the 1990s was much steeper than that in the 1980s, and the 2000–2003 period experienced a vertical explosion in civil litigation. Rather than avoid official legal systems, Koreans now seem ready to resort to courts whenever they conflict with others. Kim explained that this litigation explosion in Korea was much stronger than that in other countries. For example, in the United States, approximately 324,000 civil cases were filed in federal district courts in 2003, fewer than four times the approximately 90,000 cases in 1960. US scholars considered this a serious flood of litigation, but Korean filings increased by a staggering forty-fold during the same period.[83]

Dohyun Kim analyzed potential sociological causes, including culture, politics, the legal profession, the economy, and the social structure. He determined that the major factor seems to be the rapid economic growth, which resulted in an anomic situation characterized by the traditional culture's disappearance and the immaturity of Korea's modernization. Kim thought that, if modern rationality and legal systems spread into all areas of life, Koreans would not go to court with typical disputes. He concluded that today's Korean society does not seem to have substantially crossed the threshold into a modern society.[84]

Addressing the litigation explosion, Jeong-Oh Kim, who obtained his S.J.D at the University of Wisconsin-Madison in 1990, proposed a dynamic and critical approach to studying legal culture. He described previous studies of Korean legal culture as focusing on the conflict between Korean traditional norms and the Western legal system. While scholars in the 1970s tried to recognize the inherent structure of traditional legal consciousness, scholars in the 1980s tried to overcome this traditionalism by revealing anti-democratic and anti-national elements in current laws.

Jeong-Oh Kim criticized both groups for tending to regard Korean traditional legal consciousness and the Western legal system as fixed and finished. He insisted that these theoretical and static approaches could not comprehend the process through which Korean legal consciousness and legal behavior have changed. For example, because researchers in the 1980s regarded law as a means of governing, the consciousness of citizens could only be considered controlled and manipulated. Kim reasoned that this analysis could not explain how laws worked within a society, who used those laws, and who resisted this use. Instead, researchers of legal culture should analyze how citizens actively change traditional legal norms and appropriate the Western legal system. In particular, they should recognize that, even though Japanese colonialism introduced the Western legal system, Koreans created an independent and democratic republic by appropriating the Western concept of sovereignty.[85]

He further emphasized that the Western legal system is incomplete and problematic. Kim, who was influenced by the critical legal studies movement in the United States during the 1980s, asserted that the Western legal system developed in its particular social context with particular dilemmas. Therefore, Korean legal philosophers should not analyze the general Western legal system but should investigate the Korean legal system's adaption and appropriation of the Western system in the Korean social context. Accomplishing this requires a methodology of Korean legal philosophy, not simply a way to fit Western legal theories into the Korean reality.[86]

> In fact, American scholars of critical legal studies strongly developed the critical movement to free themselves. However, while studying their research, I was seriously deprived of my freedom and rather fell into the bondage of oppression. I tried to fit almost all legal issues into the framework of their critical theory. . . . Just as Dworkin asserted the right of equal respect and concern, we should believe that a new philosophizing attitude is necessary for Korean legal philosophers to create various specific rights in our legal reality. For this, we must create or come up with concepts that would not exist in any Western legal texts.[87]

From this perspective, Kim analyzed changes in Koreans' legal consciousness in the public and private spheres, and he explored how the dilemmas of traditional legal culture and the Western legal system are complexly combining and working in the Korean social context.[88]

5.4 *Researching Justice*

With the liberal legal system well-established in Korea, legal philosophers became interested in the issue of justice. Faced with an economic distribution distorted by rapid development, they pondered how to construct a theory of justice, paying particular attention to the debate between John Rawls and Robert Nozick. They were reluctant to accept Nozick's entitlement theory since their interest was in resolving wealth inequality in Korea's economic reality. Some political and economic institutes, supported by large corporations, defended Nozick's libertarianism. Their arguments were based on Nozick's natural justice principles of acquisition and transfer that served large corporate interests. However, most legal philosophers, who have emphasized democratization and social justice, worried that this natural justice theory would validate the *chaebols* which had grown up under the protection of authoritarian regimes. Thus, few Korean legal philosophers advocate libertarianism.

When Korean legal philosophers argue that the public interest should take precedence over the private, they usually refer to communitarianism rather than utilitarianism. Some scholars are exploring Michael Sandel's politics of the common good and Michael Walzer's theory of complex equality to break from the limits of Western liberalism.[89] They do not set Western-style liberalism as a goal for Korean society, but they also search for a new common good differentiated from Korea's Confucian tradition. Some scholars have attempted to deconstruct the modernity of liberalism through the postmodern theories of Michel Foucault and Jacques Derrida.[90]

5.5 Rationalizing Judicial Practice

Since the 1970s, a legal methodology aiming for concrete justice in judicial practice began developing in Germany. Korean legal philosophers could not pay attention to this methodology because of the historical task of repealing or amending undemocratic laws. Since the 1987 civil revolution, there has been a growing demand for judicial reform, with Korean legal philosophers making two criticisms.

First, they faulted the judiciary for authoritarian practices. For example, numerous judicial rulings contained similar sentences such as:

> If we comprehensively consider various factors, such as legislative purpose, history, and process; lawmakers' intentions; equity and justice; the spirit of the Constitution that guarantees the people's property rights and other constitutional rights; the balance between legal interests and the principle of minimum restriction of constitutional rights, etc. . . .[91]

However, most judges would not explain what is the legislative purpose, the idea of justice, or the spirit of the Constitution that led to their conclusion, failing to take the obligation of legal reasoning seriously. Legal philosophers labeled these authoritative adjudications as compelling the parties to accept judge's decision.

Second, philosophers critiqued legal positivism's role in Korea's authoritarian judicial practice. The judiciary emphasized the law's autonomy, that is, an objective interpretation and application, independent of various values. However, in the late 1990s, Korean legal philosophers contended that judges reached decisions based on their subjective pre-understandings. They argued that, in a value-relativist society, judges must explain the justification for their subjective judgments.

In this context, legal philosophers began to research the legal methodology. Sang-Don Yi, a leading scholar who obtained a Doctor Juris under Winfried Hassemer's tutelage at Germany's University of Frankfurt in 1991, used legal hermeneutics discourse theory and literary theory to criticize blind legal positivism. Based on Ludwig Wittgenstein's legal pragmatism, Yi understood the judiciary's legal interpretation as an "act of constituting or following the legal language game." The grounds for legal interpretation are acts of speech that enable the legal community to comprehend the validity of that interpretation through rational reasoning. This rationality indicates an ability to distinguish right from wrong by inference and deduction, and it is the precondition for legal discourse in the legal interpretation community. The more persuasive this rational reasoning and the more acceptive by civil society, the more correct the legal interpretation.[92]

Yi also asserted that the validity of legal interpretation in the postmodern era does not depend solely on inference, deduction, or agreement but also on emotion and empathy. Empathy corresponds to the formation of consent by rational reasoning. This subjective dimension does not mean a lack of legal justice but indicates a 'different' legal justice. We can understand legal interpretations differently by accepting literary interpretations in judicial adjudication. Where rhetoricians conduct legal interpretation, it may seem literary rather than rational, and the interpretation will represent a different world of legal justice and literature. According to Yi, the subjectivity of legal interpretation designates a dimension of legal justice realized by legal aesthetics.[93]

5.6 *Researching Applied Legal Philosophy*

Research on applied legal philosophy has recently blossomed, with scholars embracing various theories to solve modern conflicts – a distinct phenomenon in the history of Korean legal philosophy.[94] Scholars previously centered on theories of famous legal philosophers or classical themes in legal philosophy, but the approach was too abstract to address society's emergent problems. The new approach applies theories of abstract legal philosophy to specific legal problems.

For example, the Korean Association of Legal Philosophy has debated political rights and civil disobedience during the 2000 general election.[95] Some scholars have tackled the bioethics related to human embryo cloning and biotechnology[96] and scrutinized artificial intelligence and the legal system.[97] South and North Korea have had an armistice since 1953. Therefore, some scholars have been interested in peace and unification on the Korean Peninsula.[98] Korea's democratic transition did not radically break from the authoritarian past. Therefore, realizing transitional justice has not been an easy task. Jaeseung Lee has researched state crimes, purging the past, and political trials.[99] Feminist legal theory is also a major topic in Korea. Hyunah Yang studied legal feminism to solve gender discrimination in Korean society.[100] Simply put, Korean legal philosophy has sought not only to study the 'who' but research the 'what.'

Notes

1 Jeong-Oh Kim, "Beob-gwa Cheolhag-ui Gyochalo-eseo [At the Crossroads of Law and Philosophy]," *Philosophy and Reality* 35 (1997): 255.
2 Un-Jong Pak, "Hangug Beobcheolhag-ui Banseong-gwa Gwaje [Reflection and Tasks in Korean Philosophy of Law]," *Law and Society* 10, no. 1 (1994): 197.
3 *See* Changrok Kim, "Ilbonjegugjuuiui Heonbeobsasang-gwa Sigminji Chosun [The Constitutional Thoughts in Japanese Imperialism and the Colonial Chosun]," *Korean Journal of Legal History* 14 (1993): 140–72; Hyo-Jeon Kim, "Gyeongseongjedae Gongbeobhagjadeul-ui Bichgwa Geulimja [Light and Shadow of Scientists of Public Law at Keijo Imperial University]," *Public Law* 41, no. 4 (2013): 287.
4 Hyo-Jeon Kim, "Light and Shadow," 291–96.
5 Changrok Kim, "Otaka Tomoo Beobsasang-Otaka Tomoo-wa Sigminji Chosun [Otaka Tomoo and Korea under Japanese Colonial Rule]," *Korean Journal of Legal History* 46 (2012): 447–48.
6 Yookeun Kim, "Haebangjeonhu-1950nyeondaek-kajiui Hangug beobcheolhag-e gwanhan yeongu [A Study on Korean Legal Philosophy from before Liberation to

the 1950s]," in *Hangug Hyeondaebeobcheolhag-ui hyeongseong-gwa jeongae [The Forming and Unfolding of Contemporary Legal Philosophy in Korea]*, ed. Korean Association of Legal Philosophy (Seoul: Sechang, 2010), 21–23.

7 Hans Kelsen, *Pure Theory of Law*, trans. San-Duk Hwang (Seoul: Yanmunsa Publication, 1955).

8 In-Sup Han, "Hangugjeonjaeng-gwa Hyeongsabeob, Buyeogja Cheobeol Mich Minganin Hagsal-gwa Gwanlyeondoen Beob-jeog Munje-leul Jungsim-eulo [The Conflict between Power Politics and Legality during Wartime: On the Collaboration Trials and Massacre of Civilians during the Korean War 1950–1953]," *Seoul Law Journal* 41, no.2 (2001): 139–43, 177–78; Youn-Kyoung Kim, "Hangugjeonjaenggi Buyeogja Cheobeol-gwa Jaesim: 'Bisangsataeha-ui Beomjoecheobeol-e gwanhan Teugbyeoljochilyeong-eul Jungsim-eulo [The Need for the Retrial of Collaborators' Punishment during the Korean War: Focusing on the Special Ordinance for Criminal Punishment under the State of Emergency]," *Public Interests and Human Rights* 18 (2018): 148–79.

9 Dongwoon Shin ed., *Yoo Byungjin Beoblyulnonjib: Jaepangwan-ui Gomin [Byungjin Yoo's Legal Essays: A Judge's Agony]* (Seoul: Bobmunsa, 2008), 101.

10 Ibid., 112.

11 Mi Park, *Democracy and Social Change: A History of South Korean Student Movements, 1980–2000* (Oxford: Peter Lang, 2008), 61.

12 This execution is regarded as a judicially sanctioned murder. In 2011, the Supreme Court of Korea held that Jo Bong-Am had been innocent. *See* Decision of the Supreme Court, January 20, 2011, 2008Jaido11.

13 Myung-Sik Lee, *The History of Democratization Movement in Korea* (Seoul: Korea Democracy Foundation, 2010), 25–37.

14 Ibid., 37–66.

15 Hye-Ryoung Kwon, "Yusinheonbeobsang Gingeubjochigwon-gwa Ge-ue Geungeohan Gingeubjochi-ui Bulbeobseong [The Illegitimacy of Emergency Clauses in the Yushin Constitution and Announced Emergency Measures]," *Ewha Law Journal* 14, no. 2 (2009): 190–214.

16 Daetonglyeong Gingeub Jochi Je4ho [Presidential Emergency Decree No. 4], (Enforced on April 3, 1974, and canceled on August 23, 1974, by Presidential Emergency Decree No. 5).

17 Myung-Sik Lee, *History of Democratization*, 69–71.

18 A 2007 retrial found that the Korean Central Intelligence Agency manipulated this incident involving the People's Revolutionary Party. *See* Decision of the Seoul District Court, January 23, 2007, 2001Jaigohab6.

19 Myung-Sik Lee, *History of Democratization*, 91–111.

20 Ministry of Patriots and Veterans Affairs has recognized them as National Men of Merits of May 18 Gwangju Democratization Movement. *See* website of "Association of Bereaved Family of the May 18 Democratization National Men of Merit," accessed February 23, 2022, www.518kdfamily.org/stats.

21 Hang-Nyeong Yi, "Jayeonbeob-gwa Jeongui-ui Seungli: 4wol Hyeogmyeong-ui Beobcheolhag-jeog Uiui [Natural Law and the Triumph of Justice: The Significance of Legal Philosophy in the April Revolution]," *Seigyei* 2 (1960.6).

22 Jeyeon Oh, "Dongbaeglim sageon-ui Jaengjeom-gwa Yeogsa-jeog Wichi [Issues and Historical Location of the East Berlin-North Korean Spy Ring Incident]," *Yeogsabipyeong* (*Critical Review of History*) 119 (2017): 143–51.

23 Guggaboanbeob (National Security Act), Statutes of S. Korea, Law No. 3318 of 1980 (last revised by Law No. 5454 of 1997). For a critical overview regarding this Act, see Kuk Cho, "Tension between the National Security Law and Constitutionalism in South Korea: Security for What?" *Boston University International Law Journal* 15 (1997): 125.

24 Chi Hak-Soon, "Yangsim Seoneon [A Declaration of Conscience], in Gippeum-gwa Huimang Samogyeonguso [Pastoral Research Institute of Joy and Hope]," *Amheugsog-ui Hwaesbul [Light in the Dark]* 1 (1996): 67; Yun-Shik Chang, "The Progressive Christian Church and Democracy in South Korea," *Journal of Church and State* 40, no. 2 (1998): 439.
25 Dokyun Kim, "Hangug Beobchegye-eseo Jayeonbeoblon-ui Hyeongseong-gwa Baljeon [An Investigation of the Formation and Development of Natural Law Theory in Modern Korea]," in *Hangug Hyeondaebeobcheolhag-ui hyeongseong-gwa jeongae [The Forming and Unfolding of Contemporary Legal Philosophy in Korea]*, ed. Korean Association of Legal Philosophy (Seoul: Sechang, 2010), 181–82.
26 Decision of the Supreme Court, April 8, 1975, 74Do3323.
27 Jin-Chul Kang, "5.18, I Sidae Beob-gwa Yeogsa-ui Hwadu [May 18, The Hot Issue of Law and History in Our Days]," review of *5.18, Beob-jeog Chaegim-gwa Yeogsa-jeog Chaegim [5.18, Legal Liability and Historical Responsibility]*, by Un-Jong Pak and In-Sup Han, *Law and Society* 13 (1996): 308.
28 *See* Sang Rok Lee, "'Yeoesangtae Sanglyehwa'loseoui Yusin Heonbeob-gwa Hangug-jeog Minjujuui Damlon [Revitalizing Reforms (Yushin) Constitution as a 'Perpetuating State of Exception' and the Discourse of Korean Democracy]," *Critical Studies on Modern Korean History* 35 (2016): 517–27.
29 Hun-Sup Shim, ed. & trans., *Hans Kelsen Beobilon Seonjib [Anthology of Hans Kelsen's Legal Theory]* (Seoul: Bobmunsa, 1990), 10.
30 Hun-Sup Shim and Kyung-Sun Kang, *Beobcheolhag [Law & Philosophy]* (Seoul: Korea National Open University Press, 1996), 173–75.
31 Hun-Sup Shim, "Beob-ui Hyolyeog-e gwanhan Yeongu [Study on the Effectiveness of Law]," *Seoul Law Journal* 21, no. 1 (1980): 167–70.
32 Dokyun Kim, "'*Seoul Law Journal*' 50nyeon-eul Doedolabomyeo: Beobcheolhag Bunya [The 50-Year History of the '*Seoul Law Journal*' in the Field of Philosophy of Law]," *Seoul Law Journal* 50, no. 2 (2009): 78.
33 Pyong-Choon Hahm, *Korean Jurisprudence Politics and Culture* (Seoul: Yonsei University Press, 1986), 174.
34 Ibid., 177.
35 Ibid., 178.
36 Ibid., 179.
37 Ibid., 153.
38 Hang-Nyeong Yi, *Beobcheolhag Gaelon [Introduction to Legal Philosophy]* (Seoul: Bagyeongsa, 2004), 31–32.
39 Ibid., 54.
40 Ibid., 55.
41 Ibid., 53.
42 Zai-Woo Shim, "Professor Hang-Nyeong Yi`s Jigbunbeobhag-gwa Guche-jeog Jayeonbeob [Professor Hang-Nyeong Yi`s '*Gikbun* Jurisprudence' and the Concrete Natural Law]," *Korean Journal of Legal Philosophy* 8, no.1 (2005): 15.
43 Hang-Nyeong Yi, "Saesidae-ui Nosagwan Jeonglib [Reestablishing a Relationship between Employer and Worker in the New Era]," *Gyeongyeonggye [Management World]* 52 (1981): 12.
44 Ibid., 11.
45 Ibid., 13.
46 Jeong-Oh Kim, "Crossroads of Law and Philosophy," 242–6.
47 Myung-Sik Lee, *History of Democratization*, 147–56.
48 Un-Jong Pak, "Reflection and Tasks," 209.
49 Werner Maihofer, *Rechtsstaat und Menschliche Wuerde*, trans. Zai-Woo Shim (Seoul: Bobmunsa, 1994).

50 Hela Mant, *Tyannislehre und Widerstandsrecht,* trans. Zai-Woo Shim (Seoul: Mimumsa, 1994).
51 Zai-Woo Shim, "Beobchijuui-wa Gyemong-jeog Jayeonbeob [The Rule of Law and Natural Law of Enlightenment]," *Korean Journal of Legal Philosophy* 1 (1998): 27–28.
52 He particularly argued that Mencius' theory of revolution (易姓革命論) is one of the world's most ancient and the first theory of the right of resistance. *See* Zai-Woo Shim, "Maengja-ui Yeogseong Hyeogmyeonglon [Mencius' Theory of Revolution]," in *Dongyang-ui Beobcheolhag-gwa Sahoecheolhag [Festschrift for Dr. Seo Dongak: Oriental Legal Philosophy and Social Philosophy]* (Seoul: Bobmunsa, 1990). Shim wrote articles related to East Asian legal philosophy, including Zai-Woo Shim, "Sunja-ui Beobsasang [Xunzi's Legal Thought]," *Beobhagnonjib [Law Review of Korean University]* 29 (1993); Zai-Woo Shim, "Hanbija-ui Beobsasang [Han Feizi's Legal Thought]," *Beobhagnonjib [Law Review of Korean University]* 32 (1996); Zai-Woo Shim, "Dongyang-ui Jayeonbeobsasang [Oriental Natural Law Thought]," *Beobhagnonjib [Law Review of Korean University]* 33 (1997).
53 Korean Association of Legal Philosophy, ed., *Legal philosophers in Korea* (Seoul: Sechang Publishing Co., 2014), 318.
54 Zai-Woo Shim, "Samul-ui Bonseong-gwa Guche-jeog Jayeonbeob [The Nature of Things and Concrete Natural Law]," *Korean Journal of Legal Philosophy* 2 (1999): 41–43.
55 Korean Association of Legal Philosophy, ed., *Legal philosophers,* 325–26.
56 Gun Yang, "The Law and Social Studies in Korea: Beyond the Hahm's Theses," *Hanyang Law Review* 7 (1990): 6–7.
57 Ibid., 75.
58 Ibid., 76–77.
59 Democratic Legal Studies Association, "Yeonguhoe Baljog Seoneonmun [Proclamation of the Foundation of the Association]," *Democratic Legal Studies* 1 (1989): 159.
60 Ibid., 159.
61 Kyung-Seon Kang, "Haeseog-gwa Byeonhyeog [Interpretation and Transformation]," *Democratic Legal Studies* 3 (1989): 17–21.
62 Kyung-Seon Kang and Kuk Cho, "Jinbobeobhag-ui Gaenyeomjeonglib-eul wihan Myeochgaji jilmundeul [Some Questions for Establishing the Concept of Progressive Law]," *Democratic Legal Studies* 6 (1993): 295–96.
63 *See* Chulwoo Lee, "Democratization and Legal Change in South Korea: Overview," *The Review of Korean Studies* 6, no. 2 (2003): 3–26.
64 Seoul District Prosecutor's Office and Inspection Department of the Ministry of National Defense, "5.18 Gwanlyeon Sageon Susa Gyeolgwa Balpyomun [Report of Probe on May 18 Incident]," in *5.18, Beob-jeog Chaegim-gwa Yeogsa-jeog Chaeg-im [5.18 Legal Liability and Historica]*, eds. Un-Jong Pak and In-Sup Han (Seoul: Ewha Womans Univ. Press, 1995), 241.
65 Hun-Sup Shim, "5.18 Bulgisocheobun-ui Nongeo-e daehan Beobcheolhag-jeog Jaegeomto: Bunseog-gwa Bipan [Analysis and Criticism from the Perspective of Legal Philosophy on the Arguments for the 5.18 Non-Prosecution Decision]," *Seoul Law Review* 36, no. 3–4 (1995): 65.
66 Ibid., 73.
67 *Opinion of Professors in the College of Law on the Constitutional Complaint related to the May 18 Gwangju Massacre*, in *5.18, Beob-jeog Chaegim-gwa Yeogsa-jeog Chaegim* [*5.18, Legal Liability and Historical Responsibility*], eds. Un-Jong Pak and In-Sup Han (Seoul: Ewha Womans University Press, 1995), 313.
68 Decision of the Constitutional Court, December 14, 1995, 95Hun-Ma221 in *Heonbeob Jaepanso Gongbo [The Official Report of Constitutional Court of Korea]* 13 (1995.11): 90.
69 Decision of the Constitutional C 95Hun-Ma221: 90–91.

70 Decision of the Seoul High Court. December 16, 1996, 96No1892. *See* In-Sup Han, "Kwangju and Beyond: Coping with Past State Atrocities in South Korea," *Human Rights Quarterly* 27 (2005): 998–1045.
71 Kim, "Investigation," 198–99.
72 *See* Byung-Sun Oh, "Hart-ui Beobcheolhag Bangbeob-gwa Beob-ui Baenyeom [The Methodology of Legal Philosophy and The Concept of Law of H.L.A. Hart]," in *Hyeondae Beobcheolhag-ui Heuleum* [*The Trend of Contemporary Legal Philosophy*], ed. Korean Association of Legal Philosophy (Seoul: Bobmunsa, 1996); Yeon-Mi Kim, "Hart-ui Gwonlilon [A Study on Hart's Theory of Rights]," *Korean Journal of Legal Philosophy* 6, no. 1 (2003); Hyeon-Cheol Kim, "Hart Beobilon-ui Cheolhag-jeog Uiuie daehan Bipan-jeog Gochal [A Critical Remark on the Philosophical Significance of H. L. A. Hart's Legal Theory]," *Ewha Law Journal* 11, no. 2 (2007); Joon-Seok Park, "Hart-wa Raz-ui Beobcheolhag [Philosophies of H.L.A. Hart and Joseph Raz]," *Ewha Law Journal* 11, no. 2 (2007); Kyung-Hwi Kwon, "Hyeondae Beobsiljeungjuui-wa Gyubeomseong-ui Munje: Hart-ui Nae-jeog Gwanjeom-eul Jungsim-eulo [Contemporary Legal Positivism and the Problem of Normativity]," *Korean Journal of Legal Philosophy* 18, no. 1 (2015).
73 *See* Hun-Sup Shim, "Gwonwi-e gwanhayeo: Baeje-jeog Beobsiljeungjuui-eseo Poyong-jeog Beobsiljeungjuui-elo [About Authority: From Exclusive Legal Positivism to Inclusive Legal Positivism]," *Seoul Law Journal* 39, no. 2 (1999); Young-Min Chang, "Beobsiljeungjuui-ui Hyeondae-jeog Jeongae: Dodeogpoyong-jeog Beobsiljeungjuui-e gwanhan Yaggan-ui Gochal [On the Recent Sophistication of Legal Positivism: Some Considerations on Inclusive Legal Positivism]," *Korean Journal of Legal Philosophy* 4, no. 1 (2001).
74 *See* Dokyun Kim, "Jayeonbeoblon-jeog Seunginlyul Model-ui Ganeungseong [The Possibility of a Model of Rule of Recognition in the Sense of Natural Law Theory]," *Korean Journal of Legal Philosophy* 3, no. 1 (2000); Dokyun Kim, "Jayeonbeoblon-jeog Seunginyul-ui Pilyeonseong-e daehayeo [On the Inevitability of a Model of Rule of Recognition in the Sense of Natural Law Theory]," *Korean Journal of Legal Philosophy* 4, no. 1 (2001).
75 Dokyun Kim, "Investigation," 208; Un-Jong Pak, *Jayeonbeob-ui Munjedeul [Problems of Natural Law]* (Seoul: Sechang Publishing Co., 2007), 28–44; Byung-Sun Oh, "Hyeondae-ui Jayeonbeoblon-gwa Beobsiljeungjuui-ui Sulyeom Gyeonghyang [Convergence in Contemporary Theories of Natural Law and Legal Positivism]," *Korean Journal of Legal Philosophy* 1 (1998).
76 Byung-Sun Oh, "Jedo-jeog Jayeonbeob-gwa Beob-ui Haeseog [An Institutional Natural Law Approach to Legal Interpretation]," *Korean Journal of Legal Philosophy* 5, no. 1 (2002): 86–90.
77 Ibid., 109–11.
78 Un-Jong Pak, *Jayeonbeob Sasang [Natural Law Thoughts]* (Seoul: Mineumsa, 1987), 272.
79 Un-Jong Pak, "Jeonguilon-ui Inganhag-jeog Gicho [The Anthropological Foundation of the Theory of Justice]," *Sahoe Gwahag Nonjib [Social Science Review]* 3 (1983): 58–60; Un-Jong Pak, "Hans Kelsen-ui Jayeonbeob Bipan-ui Hngye [Problems of Hans Kelsen's Critique of Natural Law]," *Sahoe Gwahag Nonjib [Social Science Review]* 5 (1985): 5–16.
80 Un-Jong Pak, "Sabeob-jeog Bobsilcheon-gwa Beobgaenyeom [Judicial Law Practice and Legal Concepts]," *Korean Journal of Legal Philosophy* 3, no. 1 (2002): 61.
81 *See* Un-Jong Pak, *Saengmyeong Gonghag Sidae-ui Beob-gwa Yunli ["Law & Ethics in the Age of Biotechnology"]* (Seoul: Ewha Womans Univ. Press, 2001); Un-Jong Pak, "Beobchigugga-wa Simin Bulbogjong [Rechtsstaat and Civil Disobedience]," *Law & Society* 3, no. 1 (1990); Un-Jong Pak, "'Jeongchi-ui Sabeobhwa'-wa Minjujuui ['Judicialization of Politics' and Democracy]," *Seoul Law Review* 51, no. 1 (2010).

82 Jeong-Oh Kim, "The Normative Phenomenon of the Public Sector in Korean Society," in *Law and Society in Korea,* ed. Hyunah Yang (Cheltenham: Edward Elgar, 2013), 93–107.
83 Dohyun Kim and Sanghie Han, "Civil Litigation in Korea: Trends and Analysis," in *Judicial System Transformation in the Globalizing Worlds: Korea and Japan,* eds. Dai-Kwon Choi and Kahei Rokumoto (Seoul: Seoul National University Press, 2007), 70–82.
84 Ibid., 88–103.
85 Jeong-Oh Kim, *Hangug-ui Beobmunhwa: Insig, Gujo, Byeonhwa [Korean Legal Culture: Understanding, Structure, and Change]* (Paju: Nanam, 2006), 72–73.
86 Jeong-Oh Kim, *Korean Legal Culture*Ibid., 73–74.
87 Ji-Soo Kim and others, "Teugbyeol Jwadam: 20segi-ui Beobcheolhag, Hoego-wa Jeonmang [Special Discussion on Legal Philosophy in the 20th Century, Retrospectives and Prospects]," *Korean Journal of Legal Philosophy* 3, no. 1 (2000): 43–44.
88 *See* Jeong-Oh Kim, "Hangugsahoe-ui Gyubeomjilseo-ui Honlan-gwa Jeongseo-jeog Galdeung [The Confusion of Normative Order and Emotional Conflict in Korean Society]," *Sahoe Gwahag Yeongu [Social Science Studies]* 4 (1995); Jeong-Oh Kim, "The Changing Landscape of Civil Litigation," in *Recent Transformations in Korean Law and Society,* ed. Dae-Kyu Yoon (Seoul: Seoul National University Press, 2000); Jeong-Oh Kim, "The Normative Phenomenon of Public Sector in Korean Society," in *Law and Society in Korea,* ed. Hyunah Yang (Cheltenham: Edward Elgar, 2013); Jeong-Oh Kim, "Simin-ui Beobmunhwa (1): Beobmun-hwa-ui saeloun Insig [Citizen's Legal Culture in Korea (1): A New Perspective on Legal Culture]," *Yonsei Law Review* 8 (1998); Jeong-Oh Kim, "Hangug Beob-munhwa-ui Wonhyeong-gwa Byeonyong [The Archetype and Transformation of Korean Legal Culture]," *Journal of Law-Related Education* 3, no. 1 (2008).
89 Dong-Ryong Shin, "Beobdamlon-e isseoseo Jayujuui-wa Gongdongchejuui [Liberalism and Communitarianism in Legal Discourse]," *Korean Journal of Legal Philosophy* 13, no. 3 (2010); Byung-Sun Oh, "Sedaegan Jeongui-ui Jayugong-dongchejuui-jeog Jeobgeun [A Liberal-Communitarian Approach to Intergenerational Justice]," *Korean Journal of Legal Philosophy* 6, no. 2 (2003); Jeong-Oh Kim, "Roberto Unger-ui Sahoeilon-gwa Beobilon [Roberto Unger's Social Theory and Legal Theory]," *Oebeobnonjib [Law Journal of Hankuk University of Foreign Studies]* 27 (2007); Chun-Soo Yang, "Jayujuui-jeog Gongdongchejuui-ui Ganeungseong: Michael Sandel-ui Jeongchicheolhag-eul Jungsim-eulo hayeo [The Possibility of a Liberal Communitarianism: About the Political Philosophy of Michael J. Sandel]," *Korean Journal of Legal Philosophy* 17, no. 2 (2014).
90 Bong-Chul Choi, "Haeche-jeog Jeongui-wa Beob-jeog Pandan [Deconstructive Justice and Legal Decision]," *Law & Society* 11, no. 1 (1995); Bong-Chul Choi, "Postmodern Beobcheolhag: Yunligwan-gwa Jeonguigwan [Postmodern Jurisprudence: Its Conception of Ethics and Justice]," *Korean Journal of Legal Philosophy* 4, no. 2 (2001); Jeong-Oh, Kim, "Beob-e isseoseoui Postmodernism [Postmodernism in Law]," *Yonsei Law Review* 6 (1996).
91 Decision of the Supreme Court, October 11, 2012, 2011Du11488.
92 Korean Association of Legal Philosophy, ed., *Legal Philosophers,* 355–58. See also, Sang-Don Yi, *Beobilon, Beobinsig-ui Sahoe-jeog Jipyeong-gwa Geundaeseong [Legal Theory, Social Horizons and Modernity in Legal Perception]* (Seoul: Pakyoungsa, 1996).
93 *See also* Sang-Don Yi and So-Young Lee, *Beob Munhag [Law & Literature]* (Namyangju: Shinyongsa, 2005); Sang-Don Yi, *Beob Mihag [Aesthetics and Law]* (Seoul: Bobmunsa, 2008); Sang-Don Yi and Yoon-Young Min, *Beob Jeongsin-bunseoghag Ibmun: Hangug Yeonghwa-wa Beob-ui Jeongsinbunseoghag-jeog Ihae [Introduction of Law & Psychoanalysis]* (Seoul: Bobmunsa, 2010); Sang-Don Yi, *Beob-ui Yesul [The Art of Law]* (Seoul: Bobmunsa, 2020).

94 *See, e.g.*, Korean Association of Legal Philosophy, ed., *Eungyong Beobcheolhag [Applied Legal Philosophy]* (Paju: Acanet, 2002).
95 Korean Association of Legal Philosophy, ed., *Beobchigugga-wa Simin Bulbogjong [Rule of Law and Civil Disobedience]* (Seoul: Bobmunsa, 2001).
96 Young-Min Chang, *Saengmyeong Gonghag-ui Hyeongbeob-jeog Hangye [Permissiveness of Gentechnology from Criminal Law Perspectives]* (Seoul: Korean Institute of Criminology and Policy, 1994); Hak-Tai Kim, "Muuimihan Saengmyeong Yeonjangchilyo Jungdan-e gwanhan Beob Yunli-jeog Gochal: Beobwon-ui Joneomsa Pangyeol-e daehan Bipan-jeog Seongchal [Legal-Ethical Considerations on the Termination of Life-Sustaining Measures]," *Oebeobnonjib [Law Journal of Hankuk University of Foreign Studies]* 33, no. 1 (2009).
97 Chun-Soo Yang, "Ingong Jineung-gwa Yunli: Beobcheolhag-ui Gwanjeom-eseo [The Ethics of Artificial Intelligence: From a Legal Philosophical Perspective]," *Chosun Law Journal* 27, no. 1 (2020).
98 Tai-Uk Chung, "Rawls-ui Manminbeob-gwa Hanbando Pyeonghwa-wa Indojuui Yeonhab [Rawls' The Law of Peoples and the Korean Union of Peace and Humanitarianism]," *Korean Journal of Legal Philosophy* 21, no. 1 (2018).
99 Jaeseung Lee, "Gwageo Cheongsan-gwa Ingwon [Justice in the Democratic Transition Period]," *Democratic Legal Studies* 24 (2003); Jaeseung Lee, "Gingeubjochi-ui Cheongsanbeobli [Legal Doctrines for Purging the Emergency Measures]," *Democratic Legal Studies* 71 (2019).
100 Hyunah Yang, "Colonialism and Patriarchy: Where the Korean Family-Head (Hoju) System had been Located," in *Law and Society in Korea*, ed. Hyunah Yang (Cheltenham: Edward Elgar, 2013).

Bibliography

Chang, Young-Min. *Saengmyeong Gonghag-ui Hyeongbeob-jeog Hangye [Permissiveness of Gentechnology in Criminal Law Perspectives]*. Seoul: Korean Institute of Criminology and Policy, 1994.

———. "Beobsiljeungjuui-ui Hyeondae-jeog Jeongae: Dodeogpoyong-jeog Beobsiljeungjuui-e gwanhan Yaggan-ui Gochal [On Recent Ways of Sophistication of Legal Positivism: Some Considerations on Inclusive Legal Positivism]." *Korean Journal of Legal Philosophy* 4, no. 1 (2001): 131–48.

Chang, Yun-Shik. "The Progressive Christian Church and Democracy in South Korea." *Journal of Church and State* 40, no. 2 (1998): 437–65.

Chi, Hak-Soon. "Yangsim Seoneon [A Declaration of Conscience]." *Amheugsog-ui Hwaesbul [Light in the Dark]* 1 (1996).

Cho, Kuk. "Tension between the National Security Law and Constitutionalism in South Korea: Security for What?" *Boston University International Law Journal* 15, no. 1 (1997): 125–74.

Choi, Bong-Chul. "Haeche-jeog Jeongui-wa Beob-jeog Pandan [Deconstructive Justice and Legal Decision]." *Law & Society* 11, no. 1 (1995): 306–28.

———. "Postmodern Beobcheolhag: Yunligwan-gwa Jeonguigwan [Postmodern Jurisprudence: Its Conception of Ethics and Justice]." *Korean Journal of Legal Philosophy* 4, no. 2 (2001): 107–32.

Chung, Tai-Uk. "Rawls-ui Manminbeob-gwa Hanbando 'Pyeonghwa-wa Indojuui Yeonhab [Rawls' The Law of Peoples and the Korean Union of Peace and Humanitarianism]." *Korean Journal of Legal Philosophy* 21, no. 1 (2018): 401–34.

Democratic Legal Studies Association. "Yeonguhoe Baljog Seoneonmun [Proclamation of Foundation of Association]." *Democratic Legal Studies* 1 (1989): 159–60.

Hahm, Pyong-Choon. *Korean Jurisprudence Politics and Culture.* Seoul: Yonsei University Press, 1986.
Han, In-Sup. "Hangugjeonjaeng-gwa Hyeongsabeob, Buyeogja Cheobeol Mich Minganin Hagsal-gwa Gwanlyeondoen Beob-jeog Munje-leul Jungsim-eulo [The Conflict between Power Politics and Legality during Wartime: On the Collaboration Trials and Massacre of Civilians during the Korean War 1950~1953-]." *Seoul Law Journal* 41, no. 2 (2001): 135–79.
———. "Kwangju and Beyond: Coping with Past State Atrocities in South Korea." *Human Rights Quarterly* 27 (2005): 998–1045.
Kang, Jin-Chul. "5.18, I Sidae Beob-gwa Yeogsa-ui Hwadu [May 18, The Hot Issue of Law and History in Our Days]." Review of *5.18, Beob-jeog Chaegim-gwa Yeogsa-jeog Chaegim [5.18, Legal Liability and Historical Resposibilty]*, by Un-Jong Pak and In-Sup Han. *Law and Society* 13 (1996): 304–15.
Kang, Kyung-Seon. "Haeseog-gwa Byeonhyeog [Interpretation and Transformation]." *Democratic Legal Studies* 3 (1989): 5–22.
Kang, Kyung-Seon, and Kuk Cho. "Jinbobeobhag-ui Gaenyeomjeonglib-eul wihan Myeochgaji jilmundeul [Some Questions for Establishing the Concept of Progressive Law]." *Democratic Legal Studies* 6 (1993): 285–97.
Kelsen, Hans. *Pure Theory of Law.* Translated by San-Duk Hwang. Seoul: Yanmunsa Publication, 1955.
Kim, Changrok. "Ilbonjegugjuuiui Heonbeobsasang-gwa Sigminji Chosun [The Constitutional Thoughts in Japanese Imperialism and the Colonial Chosun]." *Korean Journal of Legal History* 14 (1993): 140–72.
———. "Otaka Tomoo Beobsasang-Otaka Tomoo-wa Sigminji Chosun [Otaka Tomoo and Korea under Japanese Colonial Rule]." *Korean Journal of Legal History* 46 (2012): 433–58.
Kim, Dohyun, and Sanghie Han. "Civil Litigation in Korea: Trends and Analysis." In *Judicial System Transformation in the Globalizing Worlds: Korea and Japan*, edited by Dai-Kwon Choi and Kahei Rokumoto, 69–103. Seoul: Seoul National Univ. Press, 2007.
Kim, Dokyun. "Jayeonbeoblon-jeog Seunginlyul Model-ui Ganeungseong [The Possibility of Model of Rule of Recognition in the Sense of Natural Law Theory]." *Korean Journal of Legal Philosophy* 3, no. 1 (2000): 65–88.
———. "Jayeonbeoblon-jeog Seunginyul-ui Pilyeonseong-e daehayeo [On the Inevitability of Model of Rule of Recognition in the Sense of Natural Law Theory]." *Korean Journal of Legal Philosophy* 4, no. 1 (2001): 47–74.
———. "'*Seoul Law Journal*' 50nyeon-eul Doedolabomyeo: Beobcheolhag Bunya [The 50-Year History of the '*Seoul Law Journal*' in the Field of Philosophy of Law]." *Seoul Law Journal* 50, no. 2 (2009): 73–92.
———. "Hangug Beobchegye-eseo Jayeonbeoblon-ui Hyeongseong-gwa Baljeon [An Investigation of the Formation and Development of Natural Law Theory in Modern Korea]." In *Hangug Hyeondaebeobcheolhag-ui hyeongseong-gwa jeongae [The Forming and Unfolding of Contemporary Legal Philosophy in Korea]*, edited by Korean Association of Legal Philosophy, 157–210. Seoul: Sechang, 2010.
Kim, Hak-Tai. "Muuimihan Saengmyeong Yeonjangchilyo Jungdan-e gwanhan Beob Yunli-jeog Gochal: Beobwon-ui Joneomsa Pangyeol-e daehan Bipan-jeog Seongchal [Legal-Ethical Considerations on the Termination of Life-Sustaining Measures]." *Oebeobnonjib [Law Journal of Hankuk University of Foreign Studies]* 33, no. 1 (2009): 311–38.

Kim, Hyeon-Cheol. "Hart Beobilon-ui Cheolhag-jeog Uiuie daehan Bipan-jeog Gochal [A Critical Remark on Philosophical Significance of H. L. A. Hart's Legal Theory]." *Ewha Law Journal* 11, no. 2 (2007): 35–48.

Kim, Hyo-Jeon. "Gyeongseongjedae Gongbeobhagjadeul-ui Bichgwa Geulimja [Light and Shadow of Scientists of Public Law at Keijo Imperial University]." *Public Law* 41, no. 4 (2013): 267–318.

Kim, Jeong-Oh. "Hangugsahoe-ui Gyubeomjilseo-ui Honlan-gwa Jeongseo-jeog Galdeung [The Confusion of Normative Order and Emotional Conflict in Korean Society]." *Sahoe Gwahag Yeongu [Social Science Studies]* 4 (1995): 93–127.

———. "Beob-e isseoseoui Postmodernism [Postmodernism in Law]." *Yonsei Law Review* 6 (1996): 187–245.

———. "Beob-gwa Cheolhag-ui Gyochalo-eseo [At the Crossroads of Law and Philosophy]." *Philosophy and Reality* 35 (1997): 255.

———. "Simin-ui Beobmunhwa (1): Beobmunhwa-ui saeloun Insig [Citizen's Legal Culture in Korea (1): A New Perspective on Legal Culture]." *Yonsei Law Review* 8 (1998): 149–94.

———. "The Changing Landscape of Civil Litigation." In *Recent Transformations in Korean Law and Society*, edited by Dae-Kyu Yoon, 321–38. Seoul: Seoul National University Press, 2000.

———. *Hangug-ui Beobmunhwa: Insig, Gujo, Byeonhwa [Korean Legal Culture: Understanding, Structure and Change]*. Paju: Nanam, 2006.

———. "Roberto Unger-ui Sahoeilon-gwa Beobilon [Roberto Unger's Social Theory and Legal Theory]." *Oebeobnonjib [Law Journal of Hankuk University of Foreign Studies]* 27 (2007): 615–51.

———. "Hangug Beobmunhwa-ui Wonhyeong-gwa Byeonyong [The Archetype and Transformation of Korean Legal Culture]." *Journal of Law-Related Education* 3, no. 1 (2008): 49–72.

———. "The Normative Phenomenon of Public Sector in Korean Society." In *Law and Society in Korea*, edited by Hyunah Yang. Cheltenham: Edward Elgar, 2013.

Kim, Ji-Soo, and others. "Teugbyeol Jwadam: 20segi-ui Beobcheolhag, Hoego-wa Jeonmang [Special Discussion on the Legal Philosophy in the 20th Century, Retrospectives and Prospects]." *Korean Journal of Legal Philosophy* 3, no. 1 (2000): 9–44.

Kim, Yeon-Mi. "Hart-ui Gwonlilon [A Study on Hart's Theory of Rights]." *Korean Journal of Legal Philosophy* 6, no. 1 (2003): 125–56.

Kim, Yookeun. "Haebangjeonhu~1950nyeondaek-kajiui Hangug beobcheolhag-e gwanhan yeongu [A Study on Korean Legal Philosophy from before liberation to the 1950s]." In *Hangug Hyeondaebeobcheolhag-ui hyeongseong-gwa jeongae [The Forming and Unfolding of Contemporary Legal Philosophy in Korea]*, edited by Korean Association of Legal Philosophy, 15–40. Seoul: Sechang, 2010.

Kim, Youn-Kyoung. "Hangugjeonjaenggi Buyeogja Cheobeol-gwa Jaesim: 'Bisang-sataeha-ui Beomjoecheobeol-e gwanhan Teugbyeoljochilyeong-eul Jungsim-eulo [The Need for the Retrial about the Collaborator's Punishment during the Korean War: Focusing on the Special Ordinance for Crime Punishment under the State of Emergency]." *Public Interests and Human Rights* 18 (2018): 148–79.

Korean Association of Legal Philosophy, ed. *Beobchigugga-wa Simin Bulbogjong [Rule of Law and Civil Disobedience]*. Seoul: Bobmunsa, 2001.

———, ed. *Eungyong Beobcheolhag [Applied Legal Philosophy]*. Paju: Acanet, 2002.

———, ed. *Legal philosophers in Korea*. Seoul: Sechang Publishing Co., 2014.

Kwon, Hye-Ryoung. “Yusinheonbeobsang Gingeubjochigwon-gwa Ge-ue Geungeohan Gingeubjochi-ui Bulbeobseong [The Illegitimacy of Emergency Clauses in the Yushin-Constitution and Announced Emergency Measures].” *Ewha Law Journal* 14, no. 2 (2009): 181–221.

Kwon, Kyung-Hwi. “Hyeondae Beobsiljeungjuui-wa Gyubeomseong-ui Munje: Hart-ui Nae-jeog Gwanjeom-eul Jungsim-eulo [Contemporary Legal Positivism and the Problem of Normativity].” *Korean Journal of Legal Philosophy* 18, no. 1 (2015): 97–130.

Lee, Chulwoo. “Democratization and Legal Change in South Korea: Overview.” *The Review of Korean Studies* 6, no. 2 (2003): 3–26.

Lee, Jaeseung. “Gwageo Cheongsan-gwa Ingwon [Justice in the Democratic Transition Period].” *Democratic Legal Studies* 24 (2003): 15–41.

———. “Gingeubjochi-ui Cheongsanbeobli [Legal Doctrines for Purging the Emergency Measures].” *Democratic Legal Studies* 71 (2019): 9–47.

Lee, Kye Il. “Sabeob-ui Minju-jeog Jeongdanghwa [Democratic Legitimation of Judiciary Power: Focusing on Personal Legitimation of Judicial Personnel Administration].” *Korean Journal of Legal Philosophy* 16, no. 3 (2013): 249–94.

Lee, Myung-sik. *The History of Democratization Movement in Korea*. Seoul: Korea Democracy Foundation, 2010.

Lee, Sang-Rok. “‘Yeoesangtae Sanglyehwa’loseoui Yusin Heonbeob-gwa Hangugjeog Minjujuui Damlon [Revitalizing Reforms (Yushin) Constitution as a ‘Perpetuating State of Exception’ and the Discourse of Korean Democracy].” *Critical Studies on Modern Korean History* 35 (2016): 511–55.

Maihofer, Werner. *Rechtsstaat und Menschliche Wuerde*. Translated by Zai-Woo Shim. Seoul: Bobmunsa, 1994.

Mant, Hela. *Tyannislehre und Widerstandsrecht*. Translated by Zai-Woo Shim. Seoul: Mimumsa, 1994.

Oh, Byung-Sun. “Hart-ui Beobcheolhag Bangbeob-gwa Beob-ui Baenyeom [The Methodology of Legal Philosophy and The Concept of Law of H.L.A. Hart].” In *Hyeondae Beobcheolhag-ui Heuleum [The Trend of Contemporary Legal Philosophy]*, edited by Korean Association of Legal Philosophy. Seoul: Bobmunsa, 1996.

———. “Hyeondae-ui Jayeonbeoblon-gwa Beobsiljeungjuui-ui Sulyeom Gyeonghyang [Convergence in Contemporary Theories of Natural Law and Legal Positivism].” *Korean Journal of Legal Philosophy* 1 (1998): 31–52.

———. “Jedo-jeog Jayeonbeob-gwa Beob-ui Haeseog [An Institutional Natural Law Approach to Legal Interpretation].” *Korean Journal of Legal Philosophy* 5, no. 1 (2002): 83–114.

———. “Sedaegan Jeongui-ui Jayugongdongchejuui-jeog Jeobgeun [A Liberal-Communitarian Approach to Intergenerational Justice].” *Korean Journal of Legal Philosophy* 6, no. 2 (2003): 295–324.

Oh, Jeyeon. “Dongbaeglim sageon-ui Jaengjeom-gwa Yeogsa-jeog Wichi [Issues and Historical Location of the East Berlin-North Korean Spy Ring Incident].” *Yeogsabipyeong [Critical Review of History]* 119 (2017): 116–95.

Opinion of Professors in College of Law on the Constitutional Complaint related with the May 18 Gwangju Massacre. In *5.18, Beob-jeog Chaegim-gwa Yeogsa-jeog Chaegim [5.18, Legal Liability and Historical Responsibility]*, edited by Un-Jong Pak and In-Sup Han. Seoul: Ewha Womans Univ. Press, 1995.

Pak, Un-Jong. “Jeonguilon-ui Inganhag-jeog Gicho [The Anthropological Foundation of the Theory of Justice].” *Sahoe Gwahag Nonjib [Social Science Review]* 3 (1983): 45–60.

———. "Hans Kelsen-ui Jayeonbeob Bipan-ui Hngye [Problems of Hans Kelsen's Critique of Natural Law]." *Sahoe Gwahag Nonjib [Social Science Review]* 5 (1985): 5–16.

———. *Jayeonbeob Sasang [Natural Law Thoughts]*. Seoul: Mineumsa, 1987.

———. "Beobchigugga-wa Simin Bulbogjong [Rechtsstaat and Civil Disobedience]." *Law & Society* 3, no. 1 (1990): 65–96.

———. "Hangug Beobcheolhag-ui Banseong-gwa Gwaje [Reflection and Tasks in Korean Philosophy of Law]." *Law and Society* 10, no. 1 (1994): 189–223.

———. *Saengmyeong Gonghag Sidae-ui Beob-gwa Yunli [Law & Ethics in the Age of Biotechnology]*. Seoul: Ewha Womans Univ. Press, 2001.

———. "Sabeob-jeog Bobsilcheon-gwa Beobgaenyeom [Judicial Law Practice and Legal Concepts]." *Korean Journal of Legal Philosophy* 3, no.1 (2002): 47–70.

———. *Jayeonbeob-ui Munjedeul [Problems of Natural Law]*. Seoul: Sechang Publishing Co., 2007.

———. " 'Jeongchi-ui Sabeobhwa'-wa Minjujuui ['Judicialization of Politics' and Democracy]." *Seoul Law Review* 51, no. 1 (2010): 1–26.

Park, Joon-Seok. "Hart-wa Raz-ui Beobcheolhag [Philosophies of H.L.A. Hart and Joseph Raz]." *Ewha Law Journal* 11, no. 2 (2007): 49–61.

Park, Mi. *Democracy and Social Change: A History of South Korean Student Movements, 1980–2000*. Oxford: Peter Lang, 2008.

Seoul District Prosecutor's Office and Inspection Department of the Ministry of National Defense. "5.18 Gwanlyeon Sageon Susa Gyeolgwa Balpyomun [Report of Probe on May 18 Incident]." In *5.18, Beob-jeog Chaegim-gwa Yeogsa-jeog Chaegim [5.18 Legal Liability and Historical Responsibility]*, edited by Un-Jong Pak and In-Sup Han. Seoul: Ewha Womans Univ. Press, 1995.

Shim, Hun-sup. "Beob-ui Hyolyeog-e gwanhan Yeongu [Study on the Effectiveness of Law]." *Seoul Law Journal* 21, no. 1 (1980): 141–73.

———, ed. & trans. *Hans Kelsen Beobilon Seonjib [Anthology of Hans Kelsen's Legal Theory]*. Seoul: Bobmunsa, 1990.

———. "5.18 Bulgisocheobun-ui Nongeo-e daehan Beobcheolhag-jeog Jaegeomto: Bunseog-gwa Bipan [Analysis and Criticism from the Perspective of Legal Philosophy on the Arguments for the 5.18 Non-Prosecution Decision]." *Seoul Law Review* 36, no. 3–4 (1995): 61–79.

———. "Gwonwi-e gwanhayeo: Baeje-jeog Beobsiljeungjuui-eseo Poyong-jeog Beobsiljeungjuui-elo [About Authority: From Exclusive Legal Positivism to Inclusive Legal Positivism]." *Seoul Law Journal* 39, no. 2 (1999): 103–23.

Shim, Hun-sup, and Kyung-Sun Kang. *Beobcheolhag [Law & Philosophy]*. Seoul: Korea National Open University Press, 1996.

Shim, Zai-Woo. "Maengja-ui Yeogseong Hyeogmyeonglon [Mencius' Theory of Revolution]." In *Dongyang-ui Beobcheolhag-gwa Sahoecheolhag [Festschrift for Dr. Seo Dongak: Oriental Legal Philosophy and Social Philosophy]*. Seoul: Bobmunsa, 1990.

———. "Sunja-ui Beobsasang [Xunzi's Legal Thought]." *Beobhagnonjib [Law Review of Korean University]* 29 (1993): 31–58.

———. "Hanbija-ui Beobsasang [Han Feizi's Legal Thought]." *Beobhagnonjib [Law Review of Korean University]* 32 (1996): 231–64.

———. "Dongyang-ui Jayeonbeobsasang [Oriental Natural Law Thought]." *Beobhagnonjib [Law Review of Korean University]* 33 (1997): 367–439.

———. "Beobchijuui-wa Gyemong-jeog Jayeonbeob [The Rule of Law and Natural Law of Enlightenment]." *Korean Journal of Legal Philosophy* 1 (1998): 11–30.

———. "Samul-ui Bonseong-gwa Guche-jeog Jayeonbeob [The Nature of Things and Concrete Natural Law]." *Korean Journal of Legal Philosophy* 2 (1999): 41–43.

———. "Professor Hang-Nyeong Yi's Jigbunbeobhag-gwa Guche-jeog Jayeonbeob [Professor Hang-Nyeong Yi's '*Gikbun* Jurisprudence' and the Concrete Natural Law]." *Korean Journal of Legal Philosophy* 8, no.1 (2005): 7–16.

Shin, Dong-Ryong. "Bughan-ui Jibdanjuui Beobwonli-wa Gwonli-Uimu-e daehan Beobmunhag-jeog Gochal [A Study on North Korea's Collectivism Legal Principle and the Rights-Duties System through Law & Literature]." *Korean Journal of Legal Philosophy* 12, no. 2 (2009):173–202.

———. "Beobdamlon-e isseoseo Jayujuui-wa Gongdongchejuui [Liberalism and Communitarianism in the Legal Discourse]." *Korean Journal of Legal Philosophy* 13, no. 3 (2010): 31–84.

Shin, Dongwoon, ed. *Yoo Byungjin Beoblyulnonjib: Jaepangwan-ui Gomin [Byungjin Yoo's Legal Essays: A Judge's Agony]*. Seoul: Bobmunsa, 2008.

Yang, Chun-Soo. "Jayujuui-jeog Gongdongchejuui-ui Ganeungseong: Michael Sandel-ui Jeongchicheolhag-eul Jungsim-eulo hayeo [The Possibility of a Liberal Communitarianism: About the Political Philosophy of Michael J. Sandel]." *Korean Journal of Legal Philosophy* 17, no. 2 (2014): 205–42.

———. "Ingong Jineung-gwa Yunli: Beobcheolhag-ui Gwanjeom-eseo [The Ethics of Artificial Intelligence: From a Legal Philosophical Perspective]." *Chosun Law Journal* 27, no. 1 (2020): 73–114.

Yang, Gun. "The Law and Social Studies in Korea: Beyond the Hahm's Theses." *Hanyang Law Review* 7 (1990): 1–17.

Yang, Hyunah. "Colonialism and Patriarchy: Where the Korean Family-Head (Hoju) System had been Located." In *Law and Society in Korea*, edited by Hyunah Yang. Cheltenham: Edward Elgar, 2013.

Yi, Hang-Nyeong. "Jayeonbeob-gwa Jeongui-ui Seungli: 4wol Hyeogmyeong-ui Beobcheolhag-jeog Uiui [Natural Law and the Triumph of Justice: The Significance of Legal Philosophy in the April Revolution]." *Seigyei* 2 (1960.6).

———. "Saesidae-ui Nosagwan Jeonglib [Reestablishing a Relationship between Employer and Worker in the New Era]." *Gyeongyeonggye [Management World]* 52 (1981): 9–13.

———. *Beobcheolhag Gaelon [Introduction to Legal Philosophy]*. Seoul: Bagyeongsa, 2004.

Yi, Sang-Don. *Beobilon, Beobinsig-ui Sahoe-jeog Jipyeong-gwa Geundaeseong [Legal Theory, Social Horizons and Modernity in the Legal Perception]*. Seoul: Pakyoungsa, 1996.

———. *Beob Mihag [Aesthetics and Law]*. Seoul: Bobmunsa, 2008.

———. *Beob-ui Yesul [The Art of Law]*. Seoul: Bobmunsa, 2020.

Yi, Sang-Don, and So-Young Lee. *Beob Munhag [Law & Literature]*. Namyangju: Shinyongsa, 2005.

Yi, Sang-Don, and Yoon-Young Min. *Beob Jeongsinbunseoghag Ibmun: Hangug Yeonghwa-wa Beob-ui Jeongsinbunseoghag-jeog Ihae [Introduction of Law & Psychoanalysis]*. Seoul: Bobmunsa, 2010.

Decision of the Constitutional Court, December 14, 1995, 95Hun-Ma221.

Decision of the Seoul District Court, January 23, 2007, 2001Jaigohab6.

Decision of the Seoul High Court. December 16, 1996, 96No1892.

Decision of the Supreme Court, January 20, 2011, 2008Jaido11.

Decision of the Supreme Court, April 8, 1975, 74Do3323.

Decision of the Supreme Court, October 11, 2012, 2011Du11488.

2 Korea's Reception of German Philosophy of Law

Hak-Tai Kim

1 Introduction

Korean legal philosophy has meaningfully developed relatively quickly since the country's 1945 liberation from Japanese colonialism. Nonetheless, it has suffered from inadequate circumstances compared to other branches of legal studies. For years, there was no academic demand for quality research, and legal studies were pursued primarily to gain employment through the higher civil service examination. Despite these hurdles, Korean legal philosophers broadened the traditional philosophy of law by discussing the notions, effects, and ideals of law; legal ethics by pursuing the substantial justification of law; and legal theories and methodologies by seeking a theory of law and understanding of legal applications.

Korean Association of Legal Philosophy (KALP), founded in 1957, marked its sixty-fourth anniversary in 2022. This small scholarly group established legal philosophy as a major discipline in the Korean legal academy. The group has progressed and maintained academic integrity, despite decades of inadequate legal education and research conditions. This chapter examines how Korean philosophers have analyzed trends in German legal philosophy to advance Korean legal philosophy since the middle twentieth century.

2 German Philosophy of Law and Post-War Trends

2.1 Radbruch's Formula

2.1.1 Statutory Lawlessness and Supra-Statutory Law

Gustav Radbruch's 1946 paper "Statutory Lawlessness and Supra-statutory Law" argued that

> The law is not merely inappropriate, but it possesses no legal quality when no justice is being pursued or the core of justice (i.e., the principle of equality) is intentionally rejected. . . . This is so because, by its very meaning, the law, including positive law, cannot be but an order and rule that serve justice.

DOI: 10.4324/9781003156437-3

This is known as the 'Radbruch Formula' (*Radbruchsche Formel*),[1] which addressed an issue raised in the tribunals for Nazi war criminals and an essential issue within legal philosophy. Natural law can be conscripted when constitutional norms betray fundamental legal principles and legislation or its administration infringes constitutional norms. Then, legal positivism and legal moralism (based on natural law) should be weighed.

The most fundamental debate within legal philosophy – between legal verificationism and legal moralism (the natural law tradition) – regards the conditions under which the law's binding force is implemented. Verificationism maintains that the law is only binding when legislated by an institution with binding power. Thus, the law's content plays no role in determining its binding power. According to Hans Kelsen's *Pure Theory of Law* (*Reine Rechtslehre*), the law may include arbitrary contents. The natural law tradition instead argues that the law's power is not grounded in its administrative force but in its content, without appeal to the law's formal institutionalization or application. Ronald Dworkin illustrated this point: if one intentionally kills one's grandfather to inherit his wealth, one forfeits inheritance rights even when there is no law prohibiting inheritance. According to natural law theorists, laws with illegitimate content never have binding force: they are cases of lawlessness, not law.

More generally, the questions seem to be: Does legislation by a legitimate institution always bestow power in a law? Does inappropriate content always strip the law of its power? To harmonize these conflicting positions, Radbruch proposed that laws lose their legitimate power only after the opposition cannot be sustained to the positive law to serve justice.[2] After Radbruch presented his formula, German legal precedents and academic theories, which focused on various issues from multiple viewpoints, were treated differently. As academic theories grappled with the binding power of laws issued by an illegitimate regime, this formula addressed the practical statutory lawlessness instituted by the Nazi regime.[3] Philosophers have since applied the formula to relieve the tensions between traditional natural law theory and legal verificationism, and between justice and legal stability, which are at the heart of theories of justice.

2.1.2 The Tension Between Justice and Legal Stability

The Radbruch Formula allows legal stability to hold a relative priority in relieving the tension between justice and legal stability. Thus, this formula presumes that the tension between justice and legal stability appears in every area of law, and the tension cannot be relieved by choosing one over the other. Radbruch recognized the concept of law as the worth of law, which is a reality (*Wirklichkeit*) that serves the ideal of law.[4] Such an ideal is understood as justice, and this ideology's content is a justification that the law aspires to achieve – the legitimate law.

Radbruch's concept of law recognizes a 'justice,' which has equality as its fundamental core, a 'purposiveness,' which extends the target areas of law, and a 'legal stability,' which demands the law's actual administration.[5] The relationship among these three elements has a dual character. On the one hand, these three ideals of law are intertwined. Justice in the narrow sense – the purely formal principle of equality – is supplemented through purposiveness. According to Radbruch's relativist legal philosophy, purposiveness cannot extend the law's content with binding force and, so, yet again must rely on an authoritative decision such as legal stability.

On the other hand, Radbruch's concept of law also recognizes the tension among different ideals of law, especially the tension between justice and legal stability. If legal stability rationalizes lawlessness and permits conditions for lawlessness, it would be inconsistent with the justice ideal.[6] The opposition between justice and legal stability, according to Radbruch, is analogous to the opposition between natural law theories and legal verificationism. The Radbruch Formula is intended to cope with legal ontology and verificationism, addressing an obvious problem of lawlessness based on epistemology. It eases the tension with a compromise: Radbruch regards justice and legal stability as equally effective legal values,[7] and, thus, his ideals of law harmonize natural law and legal verificationism. The ideal of law "is a theory of justice (*Gerechtigkeitstheorie der positiven Rechts*) in harmony with the positive law."[8]

2.1.3 The Radbruch Formula: An Appraisal

Radbruch's formula influenced the Federal Supreme Court of Germany when deciding issues surrounding the post-war prosecution of Nazi war criminals and ushered in the natural law's renaissance in the 1950s and 1960s. It also drew criticisms from H.L.A. Hart and Nobert Hörster, among others.

Radbruch was confident that the morality of legislators and citizens would improve through legal theoretic justice. Hart criticized this as one-dimensional, asserting that Radbruch misunderstood it. This moral misunderstanding might apply to legislators and citizens without legal expertise but not those who employ the law in courts.[9] Hörster pointed out that courts do not deliberate on moral-philosophical norms, as Radbruch claims, but on legal grounds. Only when moral principles have been incorporated into the practical positive law do moral principles provide grounds for judgments. Hörster's analytical legal theory questioned Radbruch's allowance for rejecting legal mandates because of injustice and criticized his approach for raising fundamental doubts about positive law's effectiveness.[10]

Hart also argued that the Radbruch Formula creates great confusion:[11]

> Those norms because of their inappropriate contents cannot be supported, if they cannot be incorporated into the laws. Utilitarianism would prescribe that the positive laws could be rejected when their contents are inappropriate. This manifests our moral judgment that everyone understands, and it thus requires direct abidance to moral norms. Such a rejection of norms, on the other hand, should not force the statement that inappropriate laws are not laws at all. The statement is either a claim that many people would reject, or that its acceptance would require so much philosophical discussions. Moral

evaluation of norms must be conducted with precise language, and thus it should not be presented with the controversial philosophical propositions.[12]

The concept of justice within the Radbruch Formula has also been targeted for conceptual ambiguity. Lawyers and citizens would probably arbitrarily rely on their sense of morality, forcing us to accept a variety of approaches to determine justice. I suggest that this criticism can be refuted. Radbruch does not reject positive law, guaranteed by institutions and powers, simply because it is unjust or inappropriate. Rather, he recognizes its legal standing. Only when its content exceeds the boundaries of justice do we conceptually clarify 'justice' by consulting the general consensus – a universal moral sensibility – about what is just and unjust. Example laws include those allowing concentration camps, slavery, genocide, sex trafficking, and discrimination based on race, origin, and gender, etc. Exposing law's characteristics responds to the criticism that 'justice' is a very abstract notion.[13]

A final criticism is that Radbruch's formula can lead to results that improperly give the law a retroactive effect (*nulla poena sine lege*) – 'without law, there is no crime, and, without law, there is no punishment' – a basic principle of criminal law. This principle conditions an act's criminality on the actor's ability to recognize illegality in advance. It was originally based on the theory of psychological coercion, where threats of legal punishment deter crime. However, according to the principle of responsibility, criminal accountability requires a preexisting basis for holding the offender legally responsible so that he knew or could have known that the act was illegal. It does not matter whether the actor could have known that the written law prohibits the behavior; it is sufficient that the actor recognizes that the conduct was against the norm's essential meaning because it was unjustified and harmful in light of relevant social and ethical values. Recognizing illegality is not a religious or other high-level ethical awareness; it regards the most basic principles of communal human life. Therefore, the norm that justifies the action refers to the most basic principle of communal human life accepted by the moral consciousness of all cultures.

2.2 Resurrecting Natural Law

Legal positivism dominated German philosophy until the mid-twentieth century, when natural law was revived after World War II. From the mid-nineteenth century, German legal philosophy followed Karl Bergbohm's thorough legal positivism. Next came normative legal positivist systems, such as Kelsen's pure jurisprudence. Legal positivism then ended, and natural law entered a renaissance.[14] After experiencing the Nazi regime, Radbruch, a leading early twentieth-century legal philosopher, revised[15] his claim that all positive laws had unconditional binding force[16] and argued that the experience with national socialism proved legal positivism a false theory.[17] However, Radbruch's argument did not comprehensively consider the historical, social, economic, and developmental factors that led to ruling system of national socialism. Rather, his was a theoretical model of legal positivism that shifted the problem and responsibility by simplifying the national socialist legal ideology as structurally indifferent to 'justice' due to legal positivism. This extreme evaluation was so dominant in 1950s German legal philosophy that no one objected to it.[18]

A new natural law discussion emerged based on lessons from that theory's past abstractions and diverse concepts. Instead of an immutable natural law and a super-temporal kingdom of values, the idea arose of a given order where the individual as an ethical person is bound. Natural law theorists tended to emphasize the ontological basis of norms and values over their contents. This natural law discourse took advantage of the post-1945 strengthening of political Catholicism and the German Federal Court's reliance on the Christian faith. Thomist natural law theory was at the core of these discussions.[19] However, a practical value philosophy was also invoked – a kingdom of ideal values independent of human values, not bound by religious beliefs, that simultaneously transcendentally grounded natural laws and justified positive law's binding force.[20]

This natural law was divided into primary natural law, which regarded the natural law's common content as immutable, and secondary natural law, which applied universal legal principles to historical situations. Primary natural law, which tried to adhere to the immutable theory of natural law, rendered the content of basic principles empty, creating a danger that variable legal principles would be understood in a super-temporal manner. This theory, which is rationally applied to objective situations, emphasized human practical reason. Thus, a 'variable natural law' theory replaced an immutable natural law and a super-temporal kingdom of values. Contributors to this theory include Heinrich Rommen,[21] who argued for the Neo-Scholastic school of natural law; Julius Ebbinghaus, who advocated existentialism; Werner Maihofer, who suggested an institutional natural law theory based on the ontology of existential philosophy;[22] and Arthur Kaufmann,[23] a neo-Thomist, who supported the historical natural law theory.[24]

Kaufmann, who understood that basic problems of jurisprudence included the ontological differences between law's existence and essence, and between natural law and positivity, sought an answer in the historicity of law – the most realistic and problematic issue in modern legal philosophy. He suggested that natural law is temporally and spatially constrained; the law has a temporal structure of historicity (*Zeitstruktur der Geschichtlichkeit*);[25] and the law must be dynamically, not statically, understood. Kaufmann saw the problem as a connection between law's historicity and ontology. He focused on how law exists purely in a factual history. Thus, he was interested in problems related to the law's ontological historicity – how the law has a history and how the form of historicity defines the law's existence.

Kaufmann's treatise, *Natural Law and Historicity* (*Naturrecht und Geschichtlichkeit*), showed that an absolutist judge cannot solve these problems. The historicity of law viewpoint destroys an absolutism that recognizes a legal order applicable at all times. Ultimately, there is no choice but to retreat to the supreme principle of the minimum and entrust the law's content to relativism. He emphasized that the law's historicity rejects extreme absolutism, relativism, and timeless legal positivism that parallels the passage of time without regard to the supertemporal natural law. Rather, we must overcome this opposition to find harmony between absolutism and relativity, validity and becoming, immutability and development, and eternity and historicity. This harmony is the basic structure of the law, the polarity of natural and positive law, and the existence between essence and Dasein. Kaufmann emphasized that these answers can be found only in theoretical differences.[26]

Giorgio Del Vecchio pointed out that "It is a contradiction to recognize the absolute. For the absolute becomes relative as soon as it is recognized."[27] Thus, mystic relativity cannot prove that the absolute does not exist. On the contrary, if there is no absolute, the relativity of cognition cannot exist. Just as motion exists only in relation to non-motion, relativity exists only in relation to the absolute, and time and history become meaningful in relation to the transtemporal and transhistorical dimensions. Law's historicity also has significance and function in a specific and historical situation, and its legitimacy is recognized when a concrete judgment is made in a historical situation.

Kaufmann maintained that the law is not merely a historical fact, where non-mental natural phenomena have no relation to history. The law's existence is determined by history, and history is attributed to law; consequently, the law has a temporal structure of historicity. The historicity of the law means that the law's essence must be found in the here and now, and transtemporal legal content is materialized in time and history and must be individualized. The truth can be determined and the law appropriate to the time realized,[28] as the law's essence and existence are always newly reconciled. Kaufmann emphasized that natural law's true meaning can be evaluated not as a complete law but as a law fitting all times.[29]

In this way, natural law discourse developed in Germany after 1945 as an alternative legal philosophy addressing the liquidation of national socialism's arbitrary domination and stabilizing the newly established German state. This theory particularly relies on Thomist natural law. The Federal Court's decisions were based on Christian natural law, even if practical value philosophy was invoked. This is evident in court decisions.

In one case, the Court ruled for a husband who did not actively rescue his wife, such as by calling a doctor, when the wife attempted suicide while they lived apart. Because Article 330C of the German old law stipulated the duty to rescue, this ruling violated the law (BGHSt6, 147). In such judgments, the Court sought to find a basis for the binding force of the core area of supra-factual law through its universal validity in civilized countries.[30]

2.3 The Existential Philosophy of Law

Maihofer developed an existential ontology of law based on Martin Heidegger's philosophy.[31] Human life is defined by self-existence (*Selbstsein*) and the existential category of 'existence as-' (*Alssein*), which is identical to self-existence. '*Dasein* in the world' is the self in 'existence as-.' With its idea of 'being,' existential philosophy supposedly can enter the social order and, thus, the legal world. The key is that individual manifestations of human beings are necessarily made in a specific social form that is predetermined by the world. In this way, along with the existential natural right of self-existence, the institutional natural law of 'existence as-' emerged as law according to the nature of things.[32]

Positivism emphasizes the law's positivity as a decisive condition for the law's existence and effect. The existentialist philosopher, J. P. Sartre, argued that "being precedes essence" (*léxistence précède léssence*), emphasizing that human essence is not determined a priori, and human existence precedes essence.[33] Humans can be completed in existence only by self-determination, not preexisting ideology. Sartre argued,

> Man does not just think that way[;] he hopes for himself[;] and he is what he thinks.[34] . . . Man is what he makes himself, and this is the first principle of existentialist philosophy. Thus, no general morality can dictate what to do.[35] . . . He can choose his own morals for himself, because man is what he makes himself. . . . Man has no lawgiver other than himself, and he freely decides on the basis of himself as absolute freedom.[36] . . . Therefore, man does not have freedom, but man himself is free.[37]

Although Sartre related this argument to man, it can be understood as applying to all spheres of human beings and the realm of law – a human cultural institution. This argument is evaluated in the legal world as an extreme form of legal positivism. Since the law's positivity takes precedence over the law's essence and content, and the law's content is subordinated to the law's positivity, the legislator is absolutely free in deciding what should be the law. Whatever the legislator clothes in the form of law is recognized as law, regardless of content and essence. Even a corrupt and immoral law is recognized as law if formal conditions are met. Thus, legal positivism emphasizes only positivity – the law's form of existence – and subordinates the legitimacy of the law's content to this form so that the law's essence is eroded into the positivity of the law's existence. Karl Bergbohm's view was that "a law enacted formally, no matter how much it has the meaning of an evil, should be recognized as binding;" there is no further consideration.[38]

In *Natural Law and Substantial Justice*, Hans Welzel argued that "It is impossible to logically deduce from human nature a legal norm of law that is independent of its existence and effect, and transcends time with respect to positive law. If people emphasize legal positivism, they will make a huge mistake and deny the existence of natural law as opposed to positive law."[39] As with one-sided absolutist natural law positions, one-sided absolutist legal positivist viewpoints deviate from the law's ontological structure and are evaluated as deviating from the law's structure in the true sense.

On the other hand, Kaufmann developed his ontology of law to overcome the conflict between natural law and legal positivism. His ontology is based on that developed from Thomism, and it accepted the meaning of *Dasein* asserted by the existentialist philosophy that appeared in the early twentieth century – natural law as the law's essence and positivity as its existence. In terms of eternity and existence, the law was understood as a reality based on the relationship between historical achievements, and the law's ontological structure was understood as a relationship between tension and unification. In this relationship, the new natural law, which recognized the law's historical limitations and relevance, pursued a concrete rather than abstract version.

Kaufmann emphasized a historical natural law created and changed by time and place,[40] not a super-historical and universal version unbound by them. According to Kaufmann, conventional natural law theory and legal positivism sought a standard of justice in the legal order and, ultimately, a final answer about what is and is not just in specific cases. Thus, natural law theory breaks from law's ontological structure by recognizing and emphasizing only the positivity of law. While natural law theory recognizes the law's essence and the duality of the law's essence and existence, natural law and positivity are both ontological structures of the law's existence. The harmony of these two aspects is emphasized by their formation as a whole.[41]

Kaufmann understood the law as a substance and tried to find its meaning from the ontological structure of this substance. The question, 'what is the law?' can be answered by the type of ontological structure the substance of law has.[42] This should be understood as a dual structure of existence. The positivity of law should not only mean the form of the law's enactment, as in legal positivism, but should have a role in materializing the law's essence. Therefore, supra-factual laws are not laws, and all laws are required to be positive. On the other hand, regarding its essence, the law is the minimum element that can exist as a law, and it is understood as the formal "ontological correctness of the concrete legal content" (*formalontologische richtigkeit des konkreten rechtsinhalt*).[43] Radbruch pointed out[44] that positive law's task is being just in content, and, simultaneously, positivity must play a structural role in legitimacy.[45]

2.4 The Border Guard Case and the Issue of Legal Effect

2.4.1 The Border Guard Case (Mauerschützfall)

From East Germany's founding as a socialist country in 1949 until German reunification in 1990, many residents fled to West Germany searching for freedom. With the exodus reaching 2.7 million by the end of 1961, the East German government built the Berlin Wall that year to avert political and economic crises. The wall hindered escapees, and border guards fired at them, leading to numerous deaths and casualties. Until reunification, casualties officially reached about one thousand, and approximately six thousand were arrested while attempting escape.[46]

Border guard shootings were a controversial issue for a reunified Germany. As courts prosecuted those who issued the orders to shoot, the legal debate over their punishment intensified: Did the border guards act legally according to East German law? Should their actions be punished? Should the government impose a political solution? To what extent can the judicial system resolve transitional justice controversies to the public's satisfaction? These legal philosophy questions required determining the basis for the law's true effect within the interrelationship among political ideology, social reality, and mechanisms for binding law.

2.4.2 The Legal Philosophical Basis

The point where criminality can be established in the border guard cases (*Mauerschützfall*) becomes clearer when considering the positive law's relevant provisions. The unification treaty permitted punishing the perpetrators in Germany under the applicable East German law.[47] The border law (*Grenzegesetz*) stated that casualties caused by intentionally shooting at border violators were justified as "extreme measures" under special conditions.[48] Absent those exculpatory conditions, intentionally firing at an escapee and causing her death was punishable as murder, but even in that case East Germany had not criminally prosecuted guards or police for killing a refugee.

Applying the Radbruch Formula, the German Federal Court rendered a judgment based on two points. First, East Germany's jurisprudence ranked Article 27 of the Act on the State Border (*Grenzgesetz*), which generally permitted guards to fire on escapees, higher than the value of an individual life to preserve the country's socialist state system. The question was whether this violation of justice was acceptable. Second, East Germany was a party to the *International Covenant on Civil and Political Rights (ICCPR)*, which provided that "No one shall be arbitrarily deprived of life." The Federal Court determined that the border law violated justice because it breached the ICCPR.[49]

However, these Federal Court decisions can be criticized. First, can the East German legal order be considered a violation of justice, which is an unacceptable conclusion under Radbruch's formula? In the Nazi war crimes trials, the main topic was the Jewish genocide, while, in the border guard cases, Article 27 required certain conditions before guards could shoot at escapees. Simply comparing and evaluating the illegality of legal content in the two cases is inappropriate. In particular, the genocide of Jews was carried out at the national level, while the provision for firing at unauthorized border crossings was the subject of domestic debate. Thus, applying Radbruch's illegality standard directly to the border guard cases seems inappropriate.

2.5 Methodology and Legal Interpretation

Nineteenth-century German jurisprudence was a reaction to the Enlightenment, which led the ideological world throughout the seventeenth and eighteenth centuries. It emphasized irrational elements, such as emotions, rather than absolute human rationality. In legal philosophy, the law's history and tradition, rather than its rationality and universality, were emphasized, and realistic research on the power to shape law began to replace rationalistic inquiry into the ideology and ideal of law.[50] In particular, Georg Puchta, a representative of concept jurisprudence (*Begriffsjurisprudenz*), which emphasized only the law's systematic aspects, argued that the positive law system has no flaws and correct judgments always can be derived by logical manipulation.[51] This conceptual jurisprudence presupposed the legal system's completeness by understanding that all legal recognition and conclusions are obtained through logical and deductive reasoning from a higher-level legal concept, and formalities are excluded from the law's purpose, ideology, value, and social reality. He argued for hermeneutics within the system.

This methodology of conceptual jurisprudence was criticized by objective jurisprudence, which emphasized a practical methodology for a realistic life rather than evaluating the law as a product of the legislator's purposeful representation and evaluating jurisprudence in light of mathematics or logic.[52] Rudolf von Jhering, a representative of the law of purpose, argued that the concept of purpose is the driving force in all human social life and the foundation of all institutions and cultures. Laws are not created naturally or unconsciously but through humans' conscious effort and activity. He, therefore, claimed that purpose is the basis of the law, the driving force of its development, and its creator.[53]

This view was succeeded by the study of interest law (*Interessenjurisprudenz*), which evaluates law by considering its generating factors – the rules and resolutions of the various interests and their interrelationships and conflicts. Interest jurisprudence started as a reaction to conceptual jurisprudence and asserted that, because the positive law system has flaws, it should be supplemented with the concept of interest in daily life. Because interest law is fragmentary and flawed, a satisfactory judgment cannot be reached only by logical inferences from existing legal norms, and supplements must address the flaws. If the deficiencies are recognized, the judge should supplement the rules by determining the interests related to the particular case and evaluate and balance them according to a comprehensive value judgment.[54]

Criticism that conceptual jurisprudence considers the law's normative effect, regardless of its meaning or practical effectiveness, and settles for the legislated law led philosophers to recognize that the law's flaws should be acknowledged and to interpret the law by analogy. This thinking confirmed the possibility of flaws in the law and drew attention to them.

The free law theory (*Freirechtslehre*)[55] appeared to address those flaws. It recognized the function of freely discovering laws or creating new laws without being bound by laws and regulations. It began by denying the law's integrity, the premise of conceptual jurisprudence. Conceptual law's legal methodology appeared as capitalism developed in the nineteenth century but could not cope with the changing social situation. Libertarians argued that flaws always accompany real law, and they criticized the formal logical method of conceptual law as a dangerous disguise that reaches conclusions through the formal logical manipulation of legislated law. They emphasized that the law would face a point where it could no longer keep pace with social changes. Therefore, the theory of freedom emphasized the judicial process' intuitive and emotional elements and insisted that judges apply the law according to justice and equity. This free law theory can be seen as liberating judges from legislated law, the dogma of the law's integrity, and legal methodology's formal and logical interpretation of the law.[56]

From another viewpoint, historical jurisprudence insisted on interpreting or discovering the law through rediscovering its factual meaning as a historical reality, while conceptual jurisprudence emphasized the law's interpretation and application from inference through the mutual subsumption between concepts. The historical school was criticized for failing to consider the law's ideology or objective purpose and mental formations, which had been merely psychological and subjective facts but were now recognized as objective and ideal realities. The ideology, purpose, and value were recognized as objective realities. Therefore, the law is not merely a historical product of the legislator but has an objective existence. This jurisprudence led to teleological methodologies in legal interpretation, expanded interpretation, reduced interpretation, and supplemented deficiencies.[57] According to the legal method's historical development, the current technique of legal interpretation is no longer profit-jurisdiction but regards the law as the legislator's value-evaluating tool, prioritizing value-oriented legal judgment. The law is understood as a semantic unity through the legal principle, not as a simple formal conceptual system viewed from a conceptual legal point of view.

Thus, legal methodology can appear differently depending on the various positions and viewpoints surrounding the law, making it difficult to determine the correct methodology by considering all meanings and harmonizing the relationships. All legal norms have a social reality because they reflect the social reality. Through this prism, the legislation's purpose can be seen as an attempt to resolve social conflicts, and the norms are interrelated with the ideology and value as a due proposition. Therefore, the correct method of legal interpretation harmonizes and considers the meanings of these various legal studies and seeks to realize the law's true meaning in a complementary relationship. Legal interpretation occurs not only through formal and logical explanation under the assumption of strict literary interpretation and a closed system of law premised on the completeness and integrity of the law's existence. Rather, interpretation considers the law's ideology and value, the proper proposition as a moral principle, and social reality. Given the law's various meanings, it is necessary to refrain from a method that interprets the law as concretely valid.

2.6 Prospects for German Legal Philosophy in the Twenty-First Century

Twenty-first-century German legal philosophy will likely further develop, and the Enlightenment natural law program, which places human dignity as the core value of law, should continue. The law should ensure that the state treats human beings with dignity, and legal philosophy should determine the law's meaning and content.

Environmental law is a new topic. Global climate change and pollution are legal concerns, and the philosophy of environmental law establishes philosophical principles based on environmental ethics, normatively empowering environmental law. Additionally, norms and ethics based on legal philosophy are necessary for life science and technological developments, such as genetic engineering, organ transplants from and euthanizing of 'brain-dead' persons, human cloning, etc. Natural law developments will address political, economic, educational, religious, media, medical, and legal ethics. Legal philosophy will develop toward restoring social morality and its practical value.[58]

3 Acceptance of German Legal Philosophy in Korea

3.1 The Study of the Philosophy of Law Begins (1945–1950s)

During the early period of Korean legal philosophy, following liberation from Japanese colonialism in 1945, research was conducted, for the first time, through textbooks and university lectures. Texts included Hang-Nyeong Yi's *Introduction to the Philosophy of Law* (1955), Hee-Cheol Chung's *Introduction to the Philosophy of Law* (1958), San-Duk Hwang's *Introduction to the Philosophy of Law* (1955) and *Report on the Philosophy of Law* (1956), and Min-Young Eom and Don-Gak Seo's translated *Introduction to Philosophy of Law of Radbruch* (1959). Publication of the *Marxist Theory of Law* (1958), translated by Kyung-Hak Chang, laid the foundation for university lectures on the general theory of German legal philosophy. While these efforts provided a foothold for research, it is difficult to say that they achieved a systematic study of German legal philosophy; rather, representative ideas and theories were incompletely introduced.

Research was also produced on German legal philosopher Hans Kelsen. San-Duk Hwang translated, among other works, *Pure Law* (1955), "The Ideological Characteristics of Pure Law" (*Journal of the Legal Association*, 1949), "Professor Kelsen's Doctrine Change and its Significance" (*Law Research*, 1954), "Hans Kelsen, The System of Thoughts in Korea" (*University Newspaper*, 1954), "Pure Law and Comparative Law" (*University Newspaper*, 1956), and "Introduction to Pure Law" (*Legal Society*, 1958). Although lacking special academic significance, they were promising considering Korea's nascent academia.[59]

3.2 The Influence of Radbruch's Thought

No legal philosopher has been more researched in Korea than Radbruch. When Koreans began studying this late nineteenth- and early twentieth-century philosopher, much relevant literature had been published in Germany. Early Korean legal philosophers, working at a small number of universities, were particularly interested in Radbruch. In 1967, Jong-Wook Jung published his doctoral thesis on Radbruch. The next generation of scholars followed this tradition, and Radbruch's legal philosophy became the most important area of Korean research into German legal philosophy.[60]

Radbruch's works have been translated in Korea, including *Introduction to Law* (1957), translated by Hee-Cheol Jeong; *Introduction to Philosophy of Law* (1958), translated by Min-Young Eom and Don-Gak Seo; *Introduction to Philosophy of*

Law (1958), translated by Don-Gak Seo and Ju-Chan Sohn; and *The Spirit of Commonwealth Law* (1959) and *The Philosophy of Law* (1975), translated by Chongko Choi. His influence on Korean legal philosophy contributed to establishing democracy. His relativist philosophies of law and cultural law helped clear the unfortunate past to overcome Korean society's dark legacies, such as a 'black-and-white' logic, disregard for humanity, and hedonism; offered a moderating philosophy during the democracy movement; and positively contributed during democracy's trials and errors and Korea's development of the rule of law.

3.3 Natural Law Theory

Korea's legal situation in the 1950s contained a large gap between the newly established positive law and social reality. While natural law returned to Germany because of the Nazi experience, Korea initially offered no room to pursue legal justification based on rational natural law given the turmoil of the Korean War (1950–1953) and chaotic social situation. However, Korean scholars soon began publishing on natural law theory.

In 1957, the Academic Foundation of the Philosophy of Law was formed, and natural law research, which had been at the center of the Western legal tradition, increased. Reflecting the chaotic social reality and opposition to the military dictatorship, interest grew in topics such as the theory of justice, natural rights, democracy, the limits and legitimacy of state power, and the right to resist.[61] Research on Radbruch became active in the 1960s, followed by several philosophical studies on natural law's renewal, including "The Return of Natural Law," translated by Jong-Won Kim (*Ewha University Legal Gazette*, 1960); "In Contemporary Legal Philosophy," by Hyuk-Joo Hwang; "The Theory of the Nature of Things" (Beopjo, 1974) and "Regeneration of the Law of Nature" by Hun-Sup Shim (*University Newspaper*, 1975).

With Korea's continued democratization after the 1990s, almost all legal philosophers became interested in natural law studies. Since the 1990s, research through the Philosophy of Law Society has been active, and the Philosophy of Law Society Monthly Reading was formed, further revitalizing monthly meetings and publications. Representative studies from this period are *The Rule of Law and Dignity of Man* (1994), translated by Zae-Woo Shim; *Right of Resistance* (1991) and *Natural Law and Substantial Justice* (2001), translated by Un-Jong Pak; and Young-Whan Kim's "Development of Political Law Theory in Postwar Germany" (*Hallym University Forum*, 1994).

German legal philosophy initially accepted natural law primarily to overcome Nazi illegality, but, in Korea, natural law gradually considered the chaotic social situation and opposed the military dictatorship. Research increased as interest grew in topics such as justice, rights, democracy, and the right of resistance. This trend accelerated when the military dictatorship was abolished and democracy realized. Significant publications by Korean Association of Legal Philosophy members included *The Flow of Contemporary Legal Philosophy* (1996) and *The Rule of Law and Civil Disobedience* (2001).

3.4 Methodologies of Jurisprudence and Legal Interpretation

Since the 1960s and 1970s, German legal scholars have concentrated on legal theory realizing concrete justice in the judicial process. Although Korean scholars did not systematically embrace this trend until the 1970s, several scholars paid attention to it when studying legal positivism.

As the demand for rational decision-making in judicial adjudication increased in the 1980s, acceptance of German legal theory and methodology accelerated with several papers published, including "Jurisprudence Methodology in the Philosophy of Law – Philosophy of Law and Rational Law," by Hun-Sup Shim (*Seoul Law Journal*, 1983); "Introduction to Law Methodology," by Jae-Sik Bae (*Seoul Law Journal*, 1983); "Ontological Transformation in Legal Interpretation," by Ji-Soo Kim (*Jang Kyunghak's 70th Birthday Commemorative Papers Collection*, 1987); Jongdae Bae "What is Law Theory?" (*Korea University Law Journal*, 1987); and Young-Min Chang's "Development of Dispute Theory in Law" (*Inha University Legal College Journal*, 1988). Hyung-Bae Kim translated Reinhold Zippelius's *Law Methodology* in 1986, and Young-Min Chang published "A Study on the Law Discovery Methodology," his Seoul National University doctoral thesis.

From the 1990s, young scholars who returned to Korea after completing doctoral degrees in Germany introduced new legal theories further revitalizing research. Representative articles are "Legal Argumentation Theory and Procedural Justice" (*Law Society*, 1992), by Zai-Wang Yoon, who began these discussions; Sang-Don Yi's "Inference in Criminal Law," which presented the dialogue theory of Jürgen Habermas and Robert Alexy; "Dialogue Theoretical Reconstruction of Prohibition" (*Criminal Law Research*, 1992); "Legal Syllogism and Epistemological Errors" (*Anam Law*, 1995); "The Hermeneutic Structure of Legal Interpretation and the Duty of Argument" (*Korea University Law Journal*, 1995); Young-Hwan Kim's "Development Process of Legal Argumentation Theory and Its Practical Significance" (*Hanyang University Law Theory*, 1995); "Systems Theory Understanding of Law" (Kyunghee Law, 1995); "Habermas' Theory of Truth" (*Anam Law*, 1995), by Jong-Pil Byun; and "Theory of Denial of Law and the Dual Value of Law Positive" (*Executives of Foreign Law*, 1996), by Ji-Su Kim.

A serious debate arose in the middle 1990s among legal scholars on a 1994 Korean Supreme Court decision, which greatly contributed to jurisprudence studies.[62] The main issue was whether Article 170(2) of the Criminal Act applied to negligently burning general property belonging to another person. Several legal philosophers participated in this debate and published many research papers.

Legal theory is far from the normative questions that traditional legal philosophy has long pursued, and academic interest has focused on formal logical or social scientific analysis and the meta-dogmatic common to individual dogmatic divisions or general dogma. However, legal theory has contributed to further rationalize discussion in the individual divisions. Additionally, research on legal interpretation and methodology now recognizes that legal philosophy covers not only abstract ideological theses but the specific details of legal practice. It has expanded the established legal practice's philosophical discourse beyond positive law. This research opened a new field for legal scholars and practitioners to actively participate in theoretical legal arguments. The basis has been laid for enabling a fair trial through discourse and reflection, breaking from judges' erroneous adjudications that have been common.

3.5 *The Development of Legal Systems for Biotechnology Research*

3.5.1 *Introduction*

Biotechnology, one of the brightest scientific areas of the twentieth century, has created hope for overcoming incurable diseases and sterility, among other maladies. Advances in cloning, artificial fertilization,[63] and stem cells hold much promise, and Korea's biotech research contributes to these advancements. While medical advances are a positive, ethical and legal issues remain, and regulations have been enacted, including in Korea.[64] Countries variously approach issues like the treatment of human embryos because of social, religious, and economic differences, but we need universal ethical standards for this scientific research. I now consider the particulars of bioethics, compare Korea's bioethics law to Germany's, and suggest reforms for Korean regulations.

3.5.2 *The Development of Biotechnological Studies*

Cloning creates a new gene set identical to the original. Some plants, such as onions, can be replicated by extracting and cultivating the root cell into a cell lump. Animal cells are also cloned and studied for diverse purposes. Controversy has arisen with using fertilized eggs[65] or somatic cells[66] for animal cloning.

Animal ontogeny is possible through female and male generative cells insemination. In 1950, an experiment transplanted a frog's fertilized egg cell into a frog's ovum, and, in 1952, a frog's somatic cell was successfully transplanted into another fertilized egg. The heredity mechanism was revealed in 1953 by discovering chromosomes' double-spiral structure. In 1970, a frog's fertilized egg was transplanted to another frog, but, at the time, the process was not applied to mammals.

In 1983, Swiss researchers cloned a mouse by replacing the nucleus of a mouse's fertilized egg. British biologist, Ian Wilmut, cloned a sheep (Dolly) using the somatic cells of a six-year-old sheep and nucleus replacement technology. A cow was cloned in Japan in 1998, and, in Korea, the calf, Younglongee, was born by cloning somatic cells in 1999. Today, cloning is done by replacing the nucleus rather than cutting fertilized eggs, and research continues. In the United States, a primate (monkey) was successfully cloned in 1966, and, in 1998, the nucleus of a woman's ovum was injected into a frog's fertilized egg, growing into a tadpole.

3.5.3 The Development of Embryonic Stem Cell Studies

Stem cells, also called 'mother' or interstitial cells, grow into different cells and organs. They are nonspecialized immature cells that can infinitely reproduce and duplicate in a culture outside the body while maintaining their unspecialized state. Cells specialize according to their development period and location.[67] The human body has two hundred various species cells, along with stem cells that are nonspecialized until transplanted to a body part. Thus, stem cells can treat an injury or recover a body function.

Stem cells are embryonic (plural-function stem cells), which can be made with an embryo, or adult (multi-function stem cells), such as marrow cells that continuously make corpuscle cells. Embryonic stem cells, also called omnipotent cells, are no older than fourteen days after fertilization and can be specialized to any cell or organ. Scientists believed that stem cells could not be isolated and cultured because they needed special devices to live outside the body. However, John Gearhart (Johns Hopkins University) and James Thomson (University of Wisconsin) each separated and cultured stem cells. Scientists now hope to use stem cells to treat brain disorders, diabetes mellitus, and heart disease. Insulin production cells can be made to treat diabetes mellitus and nerve cells grown to treat paralysis from spinal injuries. Despite the benefits, many oppose using human embryos' interstitial cells because, in the normal course, the embryo grows into a fetus.

Adult stem cells are extracted from the umbilical cord blood or adult blood, and they are primate cells before specializing into specific body parts, like bone, liver, and blood. There are hematopoietic stem cells, neural stem cells, and mesenchymal stem cells, which have garnered attention for medical materials. Umbilical cord blood contains several hematopoietic stem cells, and bone marrow contains many stem cells, including hematopoietic cells, which produce blood and lymphocyte. Proliferating adult stem cells is difficult, but they are easily specialized. They revive organs and specialize to each organ's characteristics. Ethical issues are avoided since they are extracted from adults, but their utility is low because they distribute to few parts of the human body.

Embryonic stem cells were cultivated from mice in normal diplont nuclear form, which is an unspecialized state, and their omnipotence was confirmed by injecting them into an immune-deficient mouse. In 1998, a US research team reported that human embryonic stem cells and generative cells could be cultivated in an unspecialized state. In 2004, Korean researchers cloned a human embryo using somatic cell nuclear replacement and obtained stem cells from the embryo. Stem cells were obtained in 2005 from a somatic cloned embryo created by transplanting a patient's nucleus.[68]

Embryonic stem cell treatments are useful for unusual and incurable diseases, analysis of human generation, and mass production of necessary organs. Omnipotent embryonic stem cells can be specialized for every cell in the human body. By controlling embryonic stem cell specialization, researchers can produce cells to treat unusual incurable diseases, address sterility, and can transplant cells.[69]

3.5.4 Problems with Human Cloning

Human cloning produces a person with genes identical to the original. All human cloning is embryonic cloning, limiting the cloned individual to an embryonic state. This process is used because, just as embryo abortion is a more refined expression than human abortion, embryo cloning is a more refined expression than human cloning. Embryonic cloning involves transplanting a somatic cell's nucleus into a human ovum resulting in a fused cell. A research team at Korea's Kyunghee University tried cloning a human somatic cell in 1998 and developed it to the fourth cell period.[70] Subsequently, Woo Suk Hwang's research team achieved an international first by successfully extracting a stem cell from a human embryo created through somatic cell nucleus transplantation.[71]

Human cloning is divided into reproductive and therapeutic methods; embryonic cloning is therapeutic because it extracts stem cells for medical treatment.[72] However, the two are difficult to distinguish because cells can be repurposed for reproduction.[73] The technology is divided between cloning reproductive and somatic cells. While reproductive cells are omnipotent, somatic cell's specialization is determined.

Reproductive cloning uses fertilized eggs. The egg is divided into eight cells; the cells' membranes are dissolved; the cells are separated; and the nuclei are extracted and combined with non-nuclear ova, resulting in eight new fertilized eggs. By repeating this process and freezing the ova, several clones can be created and preserved over time. Somatic cloning uses a grown somatic cell instead of a generative cell, and it is divided with an electric shock. A non-nuclear ovum is divided by an electric shock. Stem cells are extracted from the adult embryonic cell and cultivated to make bones, blood, and muscle. This method avoids some arguments against human cloning, but the research is in the early stages and has faced symptoms of rejection.[74]

Biotechnology concentrates on embryonic cloning to harvest omnipotent cells, which can be grown into organs such as the liver and lungs. With somatic technology, embryonic cloning does not pass through the fertilization process, and it uses the patient's cells to cultivate stem cells, so there is no rejection risk. Ethical and legal regulations are still needed because a human could be cloned when the cloned embryo is implanted in the womb.[75] Using adult stem cells instead of embryonic cloning avoids this issue, but that method has a low success rate. Another issue is that the embryo, whether cloned for stem cells or leftover from reproductive cloning, is destroyed while extracting stem cells. This process raises serious ethical and legal barriers for those considering the embryo a complete human.[76] Each country should establish legal regulations to address these questions.

3.5.5 Germany's Bioethics Law

Germany promulgated the *Gesetz zum Schutz von Embryonen* on December 19, 1990, to protect human dignity and life and prevent abusing artificial generative technology. Embryos include (1) a cell combined with an ovum, which can grow into an embryo; (2) a cell from an existing infant; (3) a cell, which under certain conditions, could grow into another embryo; (4) and an embryo twenty-four hours after artificial or natural fertilization (Embryo Protecting Law, Article 8). The law prohibits artificially fertilizing an ovum to create an embryo for research instead of reproduction.[77] The law further outlaws (1) generating embryos, including surplus embryos, for research; (2) abusing gender selection through selected sperm; (3) peremptory embryo transplantation without an agreement; and (4) klonens, chimeras,[78] and hybrids.[79] Consequently, procedures that generate embryos, other embryos, humans, and the dead are prohibited as human cloning.

Germany prohibits creating embryos, such as 'test-tube babies' for artificial insemination. Created embryos may be grown outside the body, transferred, and kept only.[80] Thus, the law bans research and experiments on embryos from fourteen days after fertilization and embryo research that avoids legal regulations. Violators are punished. This law, which emphasizes human dignity, is informed by the Holocaust.

Germany intended the bioethics law to protect embryos from importing and using human embryonic stem cells (*Stammzellgeset or StZG*), but a new law was enacted in June 2002 because of interest in embryonic study and recognition that Germany's embryonic law strictly regulates research.[81] This law prohibits, in principle, using embryonic stem cells, including to produce income, and acquiring stem cells to create embryos in Germany, but embryonic stem cell research is permitted. Embryonic stem cells are legally defined as resulting from fertilization outside the body and possibly specialized stem cells acquired from a separated embryo. The law regulates embryos created through somatic cell nuclear transplantation. The law permits income from embryonic stem cells fertilized outside the body for reproduction but cannot be used for pregnancy. Thus, the law prohibits income and using embryonic stem cells extracted from an embryo created with somatic cell nuclear transplantation. Fines and other punishments are provided.[82]

3.5.6 Korea's Bioethics Law

Korea's bioethics law has eleven chapters. Chapter 1 declares general rules, objects, definitions, national duty, and the right of national self-decision. Chapter 2 regulates the function, composition, and management recommended by the US President's Council on Bioethics and National Bioethics Advisory Committee. Chapter 3 prohibits human cloning and implantation in different species. Regulations about embryo generation and use, generation by medical institutions, institution and business plans for embryo studies, and agreements or withdrawals are covered in Chapter 4. Gene examination is controlled by Chapter 5. Chapters 6 and 7 regulate acquiring, using, and protecting genetic information, bar discrimination based on genetic information, allow gene banks, permit study plans, and create the Central Dielectric Institution. Chapter 8 deals with management, investigation, disusing and repairing orders, hearings, and surcharges. Supplementary rules on state aid and prohibiting disclosing secrets are in Chapter 9. Finally, Chapter 10 provides fines and other penalties.

Human cloning is defined as artificially creating a human with identical genes. From a clinical viewpoint, research that lacks safety, scientific verification, and measures of side effects are inappropriate. If a pregnancy with a cloned human is attempted without examining the embryo's growth and aging process, physical and mental defects can result, and the side effects from the birth of a human clone will be serious.[83] The law prohibits human cloning by making or implanting an embryo leading to a birth. Violators can be sentenced to fewer than ten years imprisonment; and participating in human cloning, such as for surrogate pregnancy, is punishable by fewer than three years imprisonment.

To prohibit implanting a human embryo in an animal's womb or animal's embryo in a human womb, the law covers (1) fertilizing a human ovum with animal sperm and fertilizing an animal ovum with human sperm; (2) transplanting the nucleus from an animal's somatic cell to a human ovum after removing the nucleus; (3) uniting human and animal embryos; and (4) uniting human embryos with different genetic information. Cross-species implantation creates serious issues of human dignity and value.

Human embryos have special status as potential human beings and, in Korea, gain legal status as fully human while developing. Therefore, an "act making an embryo for treatment studies," which means creating embryos for 'means' or using them as a science study's 'object,' is prohibited. Moreover, selective sex fertilization can cause a demographic imbalance in society, and, when linked to abortions, ethical problems result. Consequently, creating human embryos for treatment purposes is prohibited, and violators can be sentenced to fewer than three years imprisonment. Using a deceased person or minor's sperm or ovum is prohibited.

Embryonic research (especially stem cell research) can lead to treatments for incurable diseases, and the bioethics law encourages research with adult stem cells and frozen surplus embryos not created through somatic cell cloning. Surplus embryos used for sterility treatment will be discarded after five years and can be used for research if the donor agrees. To establish an embryo management system, certain qualified institutes or individuals must be registered as an embryo research institute, have regulated management, and not trade in embryos. The law prevents thoughtlessly extracting ovum and using disused embryos for research and respects the donor's self-determination rights by requiring a written agreement. It prohibits somatic cell nuclear transplantation for a cloned embryo except for studying rare or incurable diseases. The Korean president determines the range of study satisfying the US President's Council on Bioethics standards.

Examining genes is useful for diagnosing a hereditary disease, predicting disease, and verifying parentage, but ethical problems arise when the process is employed to determine the embryo's character traits or gender. If gene examination is freely permitted before birth, gender selection becomes more probable; moreover, determining an individual's temperament through gene examination can result in gender selection. These methods require strict control, and, thus, gene examination, which can mislead the examination receiver, is prohibited. Genetic information acquired from gene examination cannot be used for other purposes or revealed without the owner's agreement. Because genetic information contains personal health conditions, it can prejudice employment, insurance, and education.

Genetic treatment remains at the clinical stage, requiring management of the clinical process. Institutional and technological regulations are needed to protect patients' rights and safety in genetic treatments. Bioethics law regulates genetic treatment not used for reproductive cells, embryos, and fetuses.

Korean bioethics law was enacted to regulate bioethics and related security problems arising from life science advancements. Korea's life science research is world-class, but ensuring human dignity requires regulating research and experiments. Civic and religious groups claim to have established bioethics cannons. The Korean government enacted a law in 2001, and a 2004 bioethics law manages life science studies and experiments. Prohibiting human cloning and limiting an embryo's birth or management are meaningful restrictions. However, embryo management in sterility treatment remains unaddressed, and, though no statistics are available for Korea, many embryos are destroyed during that process.

While Korea's bioethics law has addressed several issues, deficiencies remain. First, human cloning (Article 11) and inter-species implantation (Article 12) are prohibited for pregnancy and research, but inter-species hybridization is still a potential problem. Creating new species can disturb an ecosystem and challenge human identity. Studies using surplus embryos can infringe human dignity. Somatic cell cloning research is problematic because the resulting human embryo could develop into a complete human with adequate nutrition and environment. The bioethics law permits human cloning (Article 11), and somatic cell cloning essentially permits human cloning because the methods are identical.

Life scientists want to conduct stem cell research, but stem cells can also be acquired from adults. Adult stem cell research began in the 1950s without serious ethical problems. Because recent reports document adult stem cells' multipotency and safety, encouraging that process may prove effective without serious ethical issues.

4 Evaluation

Legal positivism dominated German legal philosophy until the middle twentieth century, when natural law was resurrected in an attempt to overcome the post-war legacies of the illegal Nazi state. In particular, the *Radbruchsche Formel* provided a legal philosophical basis for war crime trials, and Radbruch's philosophy was actively discussed in Germany and Korea. Korean legal philosophers, who studied in Germany, published doctoral dissertations in the late 1960s. Radbruch's philosophy was probably studied in Korea more than anywhere except Germany. Around the 1980s, legal theory that German philosophers had developed since the 1970s was introduced in Korea – Korea's second generation of legal philosophy. This extended philosophical research to legal practice, a topic actively discussed today.

German legal philosophy greatly influenced the development of modern Korean legal philosophy. After liberation from Japanese colonialism, Korean philosophy was not systematic and was only partially imported and introduced. Radbruch expanded the horizon of Korean legal philosophy, and, after the mid-1980s, he contributed to its balanced development along with Anglo-American legal philosophy.

In Korea's twenty-first century pluralistic society, legal philosophy should not incorporate foreign theories simply for philosophical universality regardless of whether the discourse is suitable for Korea's legal climate. As Korea celebrates the sixty-fifth anniversary of its research into legal philosophy, studies should expand into areas encompassing the meaning and basis of law relevant to the Korean culture.

Notes

1 Gustav Radbruch, "Gesetzliches Unrecht und übergesetzliches Recht," *Süddeutsche Juristische Zeitung* (1946): 105–8; Gustav Radbruch, *Rechtsphilosophie*, 8th ed (Aufl, 1973), 339.

2 Radbruch may be the best-known Western philosopher of law in Korea because he inspired the first generation of legal scholars after liberation, as Chongko Choi noted. At that time, Radbruch was also the most prominent legal philosopher in Germany, and he employed his original legal theory to address complex post-war philosophical issues surrounding the legality of the Nazi regime. See Chongko Choi trans., Philosophy of Law (2005): Chongko Choi, *Widaehan beobsasang-gadeul II [The Great Philosophers of Law II]* (Seoul: Hakyeonsa, 1995): Chongko Choi, *Radbruch Yeongu [A Study on G. Radbruch]* (Seoul: Parkyoungsa, 1995): Un-Jong Pak ed. and trans. for *Ladeubeuluheu Beobcheolhag [Radbruch's Philosophy of Law]* (Seoul: Moonji, 1989).

3 Frank Saliger, *Radbruchshe Formel und Rechtsstaat*, trans. Zae-Wang Yoon (Seoul: Sechang, 2011), 3.

4 Radbruch, *Rechtsphilosophie*, § 4, 119.

5 Arthur Kaufmann, "Problemgeschichte der Rechtsphilosophie," in *Einführung in Rechtsphilosophie und Rechtstheorie der Gegenwart*, hrgs. ders./Hassemer, 6th ed (Aufl, 1994), 113.

6 Saliger, *Radbruchshe Formel und Rechtsstaat*, 3.

7 Gustav Radbruch, *Grundzüge der Rechtsphilosophie* (1914), 175.

8 Radbruch recognized the relative priority of legal stability over justice, provided there is tension between them, because legal stability maintains order. Because justice is formal and purposiveness relative, legal stability remains to determine the law. In this way, legal stability is endowed with power to put the law to work. The positive law's content may satisfy the demand for justice, but the purpose of maintaining legal stability may be realized simply by obtaining actuality. Thus, Radbruch emphasized that legal stability may justify the power of illegitimate laws when there is no resistance of conscience (Vgl. Radbruch, Rechtsphilosophie. § 10, 177).

9 H.L.A. Hart, *Recht und Moral* (1971), 12.

10 Hörster, "Zum begrifflichen Verhältnis von Recht und Moral," *Neue Hefte für Philosophie* 17 (1979): 82.

11 Hart, *Recht und Moral*, 42.

12 Lawyers have argued against Hart's characterization of Radbruch's view. Under normal conditions, it is common to employ dogmatic measures especially by the judicial branch. Radbruch's formula, which contains factual and ideological effectiveness, though with complexities, would not pose too great a challenge for lawyers with average legal education. See Walter Otto, "Radbruch's Formel," *Rechtsphilosophie und Sazialphilosophie* 2 (1992): 46.

13 Walter, “Radbruchs Formel,” 4.
14 Zai-Woo Shim, “21segi hangugbeobcheolhag-ui gwajewa jeonmang [Tasks and Prospects of Korean Philosophy of Law in the 21st Century],” *Ahnam Law Review* 3 (2001): 1.
15 Radbruch, “Gesetzliches Unrecht und Übergesetzliches Recht,” 83–93.
16 Radbruch, *Rechtsphilosophie*, 182.
17 Arthur Kaufmann, “Naturrecht und Geschichtlichkeit,” in *Rechtsphilosophie im Wandel*, 2nd ed. (Aufl, 1984), 1.
18 Gustav Radbruch, “Gesetzliches Unrecht und Übergesetzliches Recht,” 88; Ulfrid Neumann, “Rechtsphilosophie in Deutschland seit 1945,” *Rechtswissenschaft in der Bonner Republick* (1994), 145.
19 Franz Wieacker, *Privatrechtsgeschichte der Neuzeit*, 2nd ed. (Aufl, 1967), 601.
20 Arthur Kaufmann, “Gedanken zur Überwindung des rechtsphilosophischen Relativismus,” *ARSP* 46 (196): 553; Arthur Kaufmann, “Gedanken zur Überwindung des rechtsphilosophischen Relativismus,” *Rechtsphilosophie im Wandel*, 2nd ed. (Aufl, 1984), 51: Erich Fechner, Rechtsphilosophie, *Soziologie und Metaphisik des Rechts* (1956), 156: Heinrich Henkel, *Einführung in die Rechtsphilosophie*, 2nd ed. (Aufl, 1977), 21.
21 Heinrich Rommen, *Die ewige Wiederkehr des Naturrechts*, 2nd ed. (Aufl, 1947), 251.
22 Werner Mihofer (Hrsg.), *Naturrecht oder Rechtspositivismus* (1962), 480.
23 Kaufmann, “Naturrecht und Geschichtlichkeit,” 1.
24 Shim, “21segi hangugbeobcheolhag-ui gwajewa jeonmang,” 2.
25 Arthur Kaufmann, *Das Schuldprinzip*, 2nd ed. (Aufl, 1976), 86.
26 Ibid., 87.
27 Del Vecchio, “Göttliche und Menschenliche Gerechtigkeit,” *Universitas* (1956): 1054.
28 Kaufmann, Das Schuldprinzip, 102.
29 Ibid., 103.
30 Ulfrid Neumann, “Rechtsphilosophie in Deutschland seit 1945,” in *Rechtswissenschaft in der Bonner Republick,* Hrsg. Simon (1994), 154.
31 Werner Maihofer, *Recht und Sein* (1954), Vorwort.
32 Neumann, “Rechtsphilosophie in Deutschland seit 1945,” 157.
33 Jean-Paul Sartre, *L'existentialisme est un humanism* (1946), 17.
34 Ibid., 22.
35 Ibid., 47.
36 Ibid., 78.
37 Ibid., 36.
38 Karl Bergbohm, *Jurisprudenz und Rechtsphilosophie*, Bd. 1, 144.
39 Kaufmann, Das Schuldprinzip, 41.
40 Kaufmann, “Naturrecht und Geschichtlichkeit,” 1.
41 Arthur Kaufmann, Einführung in die Rechtsphilosophie und Rechtstheorie der Gegenwart (1977), 105.
42 Arthur Kaufmann, Die ontologische Struktur des Rechts (1965), 480.
43 Kaufmann, “Naturrecht und Geschichtlichkeit,” 28.
44 Radbruch, Rechtsphilosophie, 169.
45 Kaufmann, Das Schuldprinzip, 43.
46 http/www.jwilhelm.de/.
47 According to Article 8 of the Treaty on the Unification of East and West Germany, the offender could be punished in Germany if the punishment was recognized under the relevant East German laws, and there were no special grounds for exempting the conduct under unified Germany's criminal law. The Federal Court held that punishment could be imposed if it did not exist. BGHSt 37, 320(321).

48 According to Article 27 of East Germany's border law,

(1) Die Anwendung der Schußwaffe ist die äußerste Maßnahme der Gewaltanwendung gegenüber Personen. Die Schußwaffe darf nur in solchen Fällen angewendet werden, wenn die körperliche Einwirkung ohne oder mit Hilfsmitteln erfolgslos blieb oder offensichtlich keinen Erfolg verspricht. Die Anwendung von Schußwaffe gegen Personen ist zulässig, wenn durch Waffenwirkung gegen Sachen oder Tiere der Zweck nicht erreicht wird.

(2) Die Anwendung der Schußwaffe ist gerechtfertigt, um die unmittelbar bevorherstehende Ausführung oder die Fortzetzung einer Straftat zu verhindern, die sich den Umständen nach als ein Verbrehen darstellt. Sie ist auch gerechtfertigt zur Ergrefung von Personen, die eines Verbrehens dringend verdächtigt sind.

(3) Die Anwendung der Schußwaffe ist grundsätzlich durch Zuruf oder Abgabe eines Warnschusses anzukündigen, sofern nicht eine unmittelbar bevorzustehende Gefahr nur durch die gezielte Anwendung der Schußwaffe verhindert oder geseitigt werden kann.

(4) Die Schußwaffe ist nicht anzuwenden, wenn

A das Leben oder die Gesundheit Unbeteiligter gefährt werden können,
B die Personen den äußeren Eindrück nach im Kindesalter sind oder,
C das Hoheitgebiet eines benachbarten Staates beschossen würde.
Gegen Jugendliche und weibliche Personen sind nach Möglichkeit Schußwaffen nicht anzuwenden.

(5) Bei der Anwendung der Schußwaffe ist das Leben von Personen nach Möglichkeit zu schonen. Verletzten ist unter Beachtung der notwendigen Sicherheitsmaßnahmen Erste Hilfe zu erweisen.

49 BGHSt 39, 1(15). (21).

50 Se-Hyek Oh, *Beobcheolhag-ui yeogsa [History of Legal Philosophy]* (2012), 193.

51 Ibid., 204.

52 Rudolf von Jhering, Der Zweck im Recht (1877–1883), 87: Jonggo Choi, *History of Legal Thought* (2000), 213.

53 Jhering replaced the irrational position of the historical law school with a rationalist viewpoint. Additionally, by insisting on a practical method of purpose rather than a logical method within the system of concepts, his approach transcended the limits of historical and conceptual jurisprudence. See Gustav Radbruch, Recht Philosophie, trans. Chongko Choi (Seoul, Samyoungsa, 2011), 54.

54 Oh, *History of Legal Philosophy*, 210.

55 Both profit law and free law theory began with criticisms of formal logic and concept worship in conceptual law. Profit jurisprudence put the profit concept at the center of legal interpretation and methodology, and it sought to establish an active interpretation theory, while free law theory emphasized free lawmaking.

56 Rye-Su Kim, *Beobsasang-ui yeogsa [History of Lawthought]* (Seoul: Parkyoungsa, 1976), 130.

57 Jae-Sik Bae, "Beoblyul bangbeoblon sogae [Introduction to Law Methodology]," *Seoul Law Journal* 25 no. 1 (1984): 20.

58 Special Discussion, "20th Century Legal Philosophy: Retrospect and Prospect," *Korean Journal of Legal Philosophy* 3 no. 1 (2000): 24.

59 Un-Jong Pak stated, "Despite some vigorous introduction to Kelsen at the time, it was only a momentary atmosphere centered around some philosophy lectures, but the Kelsen School was not established. . .. To liquidate Japan's colonial legal ideology, which conquered Korea through law, legal philosophy immediately after liberation was not Kelsen's pure jurisprudence but anti-Kelsenian legal thinking."

Under those circumstances, Kelsen's legal theory was not systematically studied, and, given the limited research on legal philosophy, it is difficult to find special meaning in this phenomenon. See Un-Jong Pak, "Hangugbeobcheolhag-ui gochalgwa gwaje [Reflections and Tasks in Korean Philosophy of Law]," *Law and Society* 10 (1994): 200–2.

60 In post-war Germany, Radbruch's theory of law greatly contributed to solving issues surrounding the trials of Nazi war criminals. Even after the 1990 German reunification, Radbruch's philosophy helped resolve difficult problems with clearing the past through law, such as with the border guard incidents. Similarly in Korea, Radbruch's theory contributed much to solving legal problems related to liquidating Korea's colonial past and ending the military dictatorship that ruled the country for more than thirty years until 1987. See Un-Jong Pak and In Sup Han, *5·18, Chaeg-imgwa yeogsajeog chaeg-im [5·18, Legal Responsibility and Historical Responsibility]* (Seoul: Ewha Womans University Press, 1995); Hak-Tai Kim, "Beob-eul tonghan gwageo cheongsam [Liquidation of the Past through Law]," *Hufs Law Review* 18 (2005): 37.

61 Dong-Ryong Shin, "1980nyeondae ihu hangugbeobcheolhag-ui baljeongwa gwaje [Development and Future Tasks of Korean Legal Philosophy since the 1980s]," *Yonsei Law Review* 13, no. 1 (2006): 130.

62 Korean Supreme Court Decision (1994.12.20.) 94–32.

63 Sun-Young Park, "Gwahaggisul-ui baljeongwa ingan-ui jon-eomseong [Development of Science Technology and Human's Dignity]," *Study of American Constitution* 17, no. 2 (2006): 66.

64 Treatment developments address hereditary diseases, cancers, and AIDS, but problems include mutations, toxic or allergic reactions, undermining human dignity, infringement of human rights and privacy, commercialization of genetic information, and creating a genetic class. Korea established the Law about Bioethics and Safety (Law Number 7150) on January 29, 2004 (effective January 1, 2005) to regulate gene examination, cell treatment, cloning, and artificial fertilization.

65 Methods are divided into reproductive and somatic cell cloning. Reproductive cell cloning, which combines a sperm and ovum to produce a fertilized egg, creates a cloned organism that will be born. This research is not active because of somatic cell cloning.

66 Somatic cell cloning, which is for an existing organism, separates the cell nucleus from the somatic cell and implants it in a womb. The process has successfully cloned mammals, raising ethical problems by creating an organism identical to the original.

67 Suk-Young Hong, "Inganbaeajulgisepo-e daehan yunlijeog golyeo [Ethical Considerations with Human Embryonic Stem Cells]," *National Ethics Study* 60 (2005): 74.

68 Suk-Young Hong, "Ethical Considerations with Human Embryonic Stem Cells," 75.

69 Chul-Guen Kim, "Baeajulgisepo yeonguui gwahagjeog, uihagjeog ganeungseong-gwa hangye [Scientific and Medical Possibility and Limitation of Embryonic Stem Cell Study]," *Korean Bioethics Institution in 2002, Spring Academic Meeting <Stem Cell Study and Bioethics>* (2002): 24.

70 Complete human cloning was not done because of ethical and legal barriers. Confer: In-Young Lee and et al. *Saengmyeong-ingwon boholeul wihan beobjeongchaeg [Legal Policy for Protection of Life and Human Rights]* (Seoul: Samwoosa, 2004), 28.; Kye Won Suh, "Saengmyeong-yunlibeob-ui saengmyeong-gwongwa baeabogje munje [Life Rights for Bioethics Law and Problems with Embryo Cloning]." *International Constitution Study* 10 (2004): 114.

71 The Hankook Daily News 2004. 2. 13.

72 Therapeutic cloning, unlike reproductive cloning, is legally permitted but opposed from the standpoint of respecting all life.

73 Chan-Gu Park, "Baea bogjewa ingan-e daehan jonjung [Respect for Embryo Cloning and Humans]," *Philosophy and Reality* 65 (2005): 41.

74 Suh, "Life Rights for Bioethics Law and Problems with Embryo Cloning," 115.
75 This is the 'slippery slope' or 'dam collapse theory.' Jürgen Habermas, *Ingan-ilaneun jayeon-ui milae [Zukunft der menschlichen Natur]*, Translagted by Eun-Ju Jang. (Seoul: Nanam, 2003), 153.
76 Il-Su Kim, "Baeaui sumyeong-e daehan beobjeog ihaewa beoblyul jeongchaeg-ui banghyang [Legal Understanding of Embryo's Life and Direction of Legal Policy]," *Source Book about Embryo Cloning and Embryo Study* (2004): 160: Hee-Ju Park, "Hangug-ui saengmyeong bogje jujang [Arguments of Life Cloning in Korea]," *Problems of Bioethics* (2001): 65.
77 The process that bears a father's child without a wife or creates an embryo fertilized outside the body is prohibited. This was the first law in the world prohibiting surrogate motherhood. Article 1, clause 1, number 7.
78 Chimera combine plural embryos with different genetic information into one embryo. Article 7, clause 1.
79 Hybrids merge human and animal material to create an embryo.
80 Though less than Germany, Austria, Spain, and Norway regulate embryo experiments and prohibit producing fertilized eggs for research.
81 Regarding German law on stem cell research, see Mun-Sik Jung, "Dog-il-eseo ingan-ui jon-eomseong-gwa saengmyeong-gwon-ui gwangye [Relations between Human Dignity and the Right of Life in Germany]," *Study of Public Law* 7, no. 2 (2005): 265.
82 Un-Jong Pak, *Segye gaggug-ui julgisepo yeongu jeongchaeg-gwa gyuje [Stem Cell Research Policies and Regulations around the World]* (Seoul: Sechang, 2005), 39.
83 Article 10 prohibits human cloning procedures (creating embryos by somatic cell nuclear transplantation; implanting embryos by somatic cell nuclear transplantation; and, under Regulation 2, progressing the pregnancy of, or giving birth to, an embryo implanted in the womb).

Bibliography

Bae, Jae-Sik. "Beoblyul bangbeoblon sogae [Introduction to Law Methodology]." *Seoul Law Journal* 25, no.1 (1984): 15–24.

Choi, Chongko. *Widaehan beobsasang-gadeul II [The Great Legal Philosophers II]*. Seoul: Hakyeonsa, 1985.

———. *Radbruch yeongu [A Study on G. Radbruch]*. Seoul: Parkyoungsa, 1995.

———. *Beobsasang-ui yeogsa [History of Legal Thought]*. Seoul: Parkyoungsa, 2000.

Fechner, Erich. *Rechtsphilosophie, Soziologie und Metaphisik des Rechts*, 1956.

Habermas, Jürgen. *Zukunft der menschlichen Natur*. Translagted by Eun-Ju Jang. Seoul: Nanam, 2003.

Hart, Herbert Lionel Adolphus. *Recht und Moral*, 1971.

Henkel, Heinrich. *Einführung in die Rechtsphilosophie*. 2nd ed. Aufl., 1977.

Hong, Suk-Young. "Inganbaeajulgisepo-e daehan yunlijeog golyeo [Ethical Considerations with Human Embryonic Stem Cells]." *National Ethics Study* 60 (2005): 71–91.

Jung, Mun-Sik. "Dog-il-eseo ingan-ui jon-eomseong-gwa saengmyeong-gwon-ui gwangye [Relations between Human Dignity and the Right of Life in Germany]." *Study of Public Law* 7, no. 2 (2006): 265–94.

Kaufmann, Arthur. *Die Ontologische Struktur des Rechts*, 1965.

———. *Das Schuldprinzip*. 2nd ed. Aufl., 1976.

———. *Rechtsphilosophie im Wandel*. 2nd ed. Aufl., 1984.

———. *Einführung in Rechtsphilosophie und Rechtstheorie der Gegenwart*. 6th ed. Aufl., 1994.

Kim, Chul-Guen. "Baeajulgisepo yeonguui gwahagjeog, uihagjeog ganeungseong-gwa hangye [Scientific and Medical Possibility and Limitation of Embryonic Stem Cell Study]." *Korean Bioethics Institution in 2002, Spring Academic Meeting <Stem Cell Study and Bioethics>* (2002): 24–25.

Kim, Hak-Tai. "Beob-eul tonghan gwageo cheongsan [Liquidation of the Past through Law]." *Hufs Law Review* 18 (2005): 27–54.

Kim, Rye-Su. *Beobsasang-ui yeogsa [History of Lawthought]*. Seoul: Parkyoungsa, 1976.

Lee, In-Young and et al. *Saengmyeong-ingwon boholeul wihan beobjeongchaeg [Legal Policy for Protection of Life and Human Rights]*. Seoul: Samwoosa, 2004.

Maihofer, Werner. *Recht und Sein*, 1954.

———, (Hrsg.). *Naturrecht oder Rechtspositivismus*, 1962.

Neumann, Ulfrid. *Rechtsphilosophie in Deutschland seit 1945, Rechtswissenschaft in der Bonner Republick*, 1994.

Oh, Se-Hyek. *Beobcheolhag-ui yeogsa [History of Legal Philosophy]*. Seoul: Sechang, 2012.

Otto, Walter. "Radbruchs Formel." Translated by Jeong-Hoon Park *Rechtsphilosophie und Sazialphilosophie Vol. 2*, Seoul, Kyoyookbook (1992): 29–54.

Pak, Un-Jong. "Hangugbeobcheolhag-ui gochalgwa gwaje [Reflections and Tasks in Korean Philosophy of Law]." *Law and Society* 10 (1994): 189–223.

———. *Segye gaggug-ui julgisepo yeongu jeongchaeg-gwa gyuje [Stem Cell Research Policies and Regulations around the World]*. Seoul: Sechang, 2005.

Pak, Un-Jong, and In Sup Han. *5·18, Chaeg-imgwa yeogsajeog chaeg-im [5·18, Liability and Historical Responsibility]*. Seoul: Ewha Womans University Press, 1995.

Park, Chan-Gu. "Baea bogjewa ingan-e daehan jonjung [Respect for Embryo Cloning and Humans]." *Philosophy and Reality* 65 (2005): 39–50.

Park, Sun-Young. "Gwahaggisul-ui baljeongwa ingan-ui jon-eomseong [Development of Science Technology and Human's Dignity]." *Study of American Constitution* 17, no. 2 (2006): 165–213.

Radbruch, Gustav. *Grundzüge der Rechtsphilosophie*, 1914.

———. *Rechtsphilosophie*. 3rd ed. Aufl., 1932.

———. *Rechtsphilosophie*. 8th ed. Aufl., 1973.

Rommen, Heinrich. *Die ewige Wiederkehr des Naturrechts*. 2nd ed. Aufl., 1947.

Saliger, Frank. *Radbruchshe Formel Und Rechtsstaat*. Translated by Jae-Wang Yun. Seoul: Sechang, 2011.

Sartre, Jean-Paul. *L'existentialisme est un humanism*, 1946.

Shim, Zai-Woo. "21segi hangugbeobcheolhag-ui gwajewa jeonmang [Tasks and Prospects of Korean Philosophy of Law in the 21st Century]." *Ahnam Law Review* 13 (2001): 1–11.

Shin, Dong-Ryong. "1980nyeondae ihu hangugbeobcheolhag-ui baljeongwa gwaje [Development and Future Tasks of Korean Legal Philosophy since the 1980s]." *Yonsei Law Review* 13, no. 1 (2006): 123–55.

Suh, Kye Won. "Saengmyeong-yunlibeob-ui saengmyeong-gwongwa baeabogje munje [Life Rights for Bioethics Law and Problems with Embryo Cloning]." *International Constitution Study* 10 (2004): 113–44.

Wieacker, Franz. *Privatrechtsgeschichte der Neuzeit*. 2nd ed. Aufl., 1967.

3 Acceptance of Anglo-American Jurisprudence

Joon-Seok Park

1 Introduction

This chapter describes the influence of Anglo-American jurisprudence on Korea's modern philosophy of law. The United States Army's military government in Korea (USAMGIK) introduced common law and initiated a nationwide boom in American jurisprudence. This wave gradually declined, replaced in the 1960s by a rush toward mainly German jurisprudence with a civil law system very similar to what Japan transplanted to Korea during colonialism. This chapter discusses some outstanding scholars from this early stage of Korean legal philosophy, including Paul K. Ryu and Pyong-Choon Hahm (section 2).

Later, a lively interest in common law jurisprudence returned to Korea, as Anglo-American legal theorists came to occupy dominant positions in global academia. They included British jurisprudence, represented by H.L.A. Hart's legacy (subsection 3.1); American jurisprudence, including pragmatism, legal realism, and critical legal studies (subsection 3.2); and the new anti-positivist movement with the debates between Hart and Lon L. Fuller and between Hart and Ronald Dworkin (subsection 3.3).

This chapter demonstrates that Anglo-American jurisprudence has influenced Korea's public law rather than private law. I also argue that American jurisprudence's interdisciplinary trend should take root in Korean academia, especially after the country introduced the 'law school system' in 2009, and Korea's new anti-positivist legal theories should more practically incorporate a 'participatory perspective.'

Finally, I suggest that normative gaps between the positivist sources thesis and anti-positivist moral requirements may soon be considered foundations of law demanding attention from Korean and global academia. If the law is not simply a fixed precondition of social development but an evolving social entity, those normative gaps may manifest the law's trajectory and drive social movements.

2 Culture and Science

Korean legal scholars learned from their country's experience with legal transplantation that conflicts between cultural traditions and newly introduced

DOI: 10.4324/9781003156437-4

modern law should be taken seriously. In the early twentieth century, Japanese colonialism forced Korea to accept the civil law system, and, before long, another political change became inevitable when Japan was defeated. In 1945, Korea was liberated, and the USAMGIK initiated its interim regime. After a year, in November 1946, the Korean-American Legal Academy was established; the following year, in May 1947, the first judicial envoy, consisting mainly of legal professionals, was dispatched to observe the United States' criminal justice system and legal institutions.[1] These events are critical for contemporary legal historians to understand the common law system's transplantation and how it influenced Korea's modern republic.[2]

Early interest in the normative setting of common law countries motivated a few young aspiring scholars to study law in American universities and return dedicated to developing legal research, education, and the law. This favorable scholarly attention culminated with the Korean Legal Center's (KLC) establishment in 1956 and many academic societies, including the Korean Association of Legal Philosophy, a year after.[3] The KLC, renamed the Korean Society of Law (KSL) in 2018, described its purpose:

> Korea was in dire need of the democratic rule of law and the establishment of a modern legal system. Further, the country was caught in a transitional phenomenon. The Korean legal system was based on the civil law system and its founding theories. Most legal professionals did not have the resources to familiarize themselves with Anglo-American law as the counterpart of civil law, and with other foreign laws. The civil law system and its theoretical outcomes, however, failed to match actual cases. By integrating Anglo-American law that emphasizes the appropriate application of rules and principles, and other foreign laws, it would be possible for us to create a complete, more balanced legal order in Korea. With the support of our American peers, the Korean Society of Law was established as a joint research organization by and in support of Korean legal professionals.[4]

These heroic scholars were attracted by the idea of culture and the scientific method for their research. Initially, the idea of culture moderated the pressure from modern Western rules colliding with Korea's traditional ways. For instance, the *Criminal Act* (1953) provides that a "justifiable act" is "an act, which is conducted in accordance with rules of law, or in pursuance of accepted business practices, or other act, which does not violate the social norms," and that such an act "shall not be punished."[5] Though still a controversial interpretation, this language indicates that "social norms" can justify certain statutorily prohibited criminal conduct, not otherwise excused by positive sources of law. As the shared standards of acceptable behavior, social norms (good manners and morals) are construed as part of the criteria for deciding an act's illegality:

> Article 20 of the *Criminal Act*, which stipulates that acts that do not violate social norms are not punished, is based on the concept of social norms as

> the most basic standard for judging illegality. Accordingly, even when an act seems to conform to the description of criminal conduct in the statutes, the illegality is eliminated and cannot be punished only if it is considered to be one of the extremely normal forms of life and within the scope of the historically created order of social life. What is supposed to be punished by statutes is not construed as violating social norms only if, as a result of social development, it is accepted to be licit and its punishment is considered not only worthless but contrary to social justice, or it realizes a social value given the goals of a liberal democratic society.[6]

After South Korea became a newly independent republic, legislators intended to preserve social norms inherited from the country's traditional modus vivendi while encouraging progress toward a modern standard of living.[7] Presumably, they believed that these norms constituted part of their cultural identity and it would be unintelligible to judge illegal any act guided by these norms, although statutorily a crime.[8]

Meanwhile, the idea of culture was related to something far more important that should concern Korean scholars – achieving the rule of law while reconstructing the country. In this regard, the rule of law has been thought to imply both that state powers should be exercised based on laws and that society's members are primarily accountable to legal rules.[9] Asian countries' culture has often been considered a major reason for failing to achieve the rule of law. Thus, a pressing issue for numerous legal scholars in Asia is unraveling cultural mysteries. In this context, culture is no longer merely a moderator or buffer reducing friction among disparate and usually incommensurate elements in a heterogeneous legal scheme. Rather, it becomes a catalyst for a series of engagements in political discourse, where battle cries like "Asian values," "Confucian democracy," and "East Asian jurisprudence" have been raised.

During the 1950s, Korea had to focus on overhauling its legal system, even amidst the Korean War. Consequently, legal scholars "could not afford to turn their eyes to the acceptance and digestion of new foreign theories,"[10] so there was no substantial change in the method of jurisprudence. According to a legal historian, Korean jurisprudence was "dominated by legal positivism, or the so-called conceptual jurisprudence, due to the influence of Japan."[11]

Around the 1960s, scholars returning from studies in the United States became the leading exponents of the scientific method of legal research, a unique feature of American legal studies. They sought to connect knowledge and insight from modern sciences, for instance, psychology and anthropology, with their analysis and critique of legal issues. They realized that scientific understanding of reality was fundamental to addressing various legal questions:

> Such methods of reasoning tend to obscure the realities of the psychological and social situation which should be considered in determining questions such as, what ought to be the basis and scope of an "accomplice's" responsibility, what is the proper philosophy of self-defense and of the defense of others and

> under what circumstances a pertinent "defense" quality should be affirmed. We must not forget that "complicity" is a *sui generis* social and psychological phenomenon, which has not been as yet "scientifically" fully evaluated.[12]
>
> In any "scientific" research, the methodology adopted is of crucial importance. We have adopted a methodology that seemed under the circumstances most objective and feasible.[13]

Paul K. Ryu and Pyong-Choon Hahm were the torchbearers for this evolving method of jurisprudence. Several scholars have pointed out that the New Haven school of jurisprudence greatly influenced these two outstanding forerunners' academic growth.[14] Admittedly, from the point of view of law as policy science, one of the most prominent contributions from the neo-realism of Myres S. McDougal and Harold D. Lasswell was to emphasize grounding public policy in a scientific understanding of social reality.

Ryu wrote his 1958 J.S.D. dissertation under the supervision of McDougal and F.S.C. Northrop. He interacted with "one of the first scholars to use Freudian insights in the study of political behavior,"[15] which may, at least partially, explain placing such importance on depth psychology, rather than other disciplines, as a methodological basis of jurisprudence.

From 1966 to 1968, Hahm was a Fulbright Research Scholar at Yale, but, years earlier, he conducted a "nationwide social survey" as part of a significant empirical project.[16] However, the policy science of neo-realism seems to have reinforced his ideas concerning the tension between tradition and modernity and their necessary reduction for Korea's development.[17]

2.1 Paul K. Ryu (1915–1998)

Ever since Ryu's 1958 J.S.D. dissertation, entitled "Korean Culture and Criminal Responsibility – An Application of a Scientific Approach to Law," his characteristic method can be summarized as linguistic symbolism and depth psychology. The former relates to laws and legal concepts put in a linguistic form, while the latter primarily concerns persons to whom the law applies. Concurrently, the law is and should be based on a knowledge and understanding of human nature, especially "the operations of the human mind,"[18] because people must understand the law's language to follow it. Therefore, linguistic symbolism and depth psychology are inextricably intertwined in Ryu's scientific method of jurisprudence.

Ryu's critique of "normative Schuld" reveals this methodology. If "reasonableness (*zumutbarkeit*), alone, determined criminal responsibility," an escaping prisoner would not be criminally responsible for the escape[19] since pursuing one's freedom is never unreasonable.[20] Construing criminal responsibility as any one factor is superficial. Rather, criminal law is a multilayered fabric[21] presenting a multifaceted configuration[22] that retains a depth to be explored.

The main reason for criminal law's multidimensional structure is that language composes it.[23] The linguistic surface may conceal a bundle of meanings in criminal law's doctrines and provisions.[24] Following C. S. Peirce's assortment of signs, language is a sign whose "competence as a vehicle for meaning"[25] is granted by convention. Language is a symbol whose relationship with its object is arbitrary by nature.[26] A concept's meaning in a specific context is determined by its background symbolic structure[27] and reveals itself differently depending on the situation.

To support his linguistic symbolism, Ryu referred to McDougal, Lasswell, and Northrop, along with A. N. Whitehead and B. L. Whorf. Language's symbolic implications are transmitted to users (people) through a Freudian approach to the symbolic meanings of basic words.[28] Linguistics and psychology, as the bases of his method of jurisprudence, now converged under the banner of symbolism.[29]

Ryu traced his methodological focus on depth psychology to Helen Silving's acute insights.[30] He concentrated on the unconscious to redefine the nature of criminal responsibility and readjust the state's sanction policy.[31] This hugely ambitious project was facilitated by Lasswell's scrupulous approach to policy based on a scientific understanding of reality:[32]

> While a large variety of "sciences" may be involved in legal situations, there is one science that is involved in all such situations. That science is psychology.[33]

Ryu's meaning, however, did not clearly come across. Korean scholars from multiple disciplines critiqued his dissertation.[34] His project sparked debates over his method of jurisprudence, especially its feasibility as a cornerstone of criminal law, known for demanding the most rigorous approach.[35] According to his critics, Freudian ideas of the unconscious, the "penumbra situation,"[36] symbolic analysis, etc. undermine criminal law's objectivity and stability.

Ryu responded to his critics:

> Conventional law is structured on a number of psychologically unrealistic assumptions: that mental phenomena are exclusively conscious or preconscious; that each conduct is referable exclusively to one particular simple phenomenon of "intent;" and that in fact it may be ascribed to a particular compartment within the human mind, reason, will, or emotion. But while these assumptions are maintained, certain aspects of law seem to indicate that law is not entirely blind to the impact of unconscious forces upon human action. . . . But since in law recognition of the role of the Unconscious is itself unconscious, it often operates irrationally. There is no clear, verbalized and conceptualized policy guiding such recognition. A conscious policy reached against the background of scientific knowledge rather than an unconscious groping for an intuitively "right" decision is the essence of statesmanship in the criminal law of a free society.[37]

As a legal philosopher and criminal law expert, Young-Min Chang, reminds us that Ryu strove to explain "the phenomena that criminal law already has taken the unconscious into consideration without realizing it."[38] Ryu explored reconciling theory's coherence and flexibility, for instance, his "teleological theory of causation"[39] and "penumbra situation" approach to the issue of *actio libera in causa*.[40] Chang urges a reappraisal of Ryu's project and argues that his method of jurisprudence does not undermine the rule of law and its stability.[41]

Ryu emphasized that researchers must employ the right methodology for studying a problem. "It is the problem that designates the method and not vice versa," observed Ryu, with a conviction consistent with the views of John Dewey and Northrop.[42] His first problem was the same one his colleagues faced – rebuilding Korea from ruins: "We must first accurately understand the social heredity of our society and lay the foundation for the reconstruction of Korea."[43] He considered the rule of law central to national prosperity and world peace, or, as Roscoe Pound put it, a "justice according to law."[44]

Symbolism, for Ryu, was a door simultaneously opening into the past and future, bridging the gap between tradition and modernity by giving voice to culture, religion, and ethnic experiences. However, his primary goal was always the rule of law, not the rule of culture as the rule of "the unconscious." The road through the past's charred remains to a future "free society" that respects human dignity[45] emerges in this lone scholar still living in us today.

2.2 Pyong-Choon Hahm (1932–1983)

Hahm began his career as a legal scholar in 1959, shortly after obtaining a J.D.[46] His writings published or drafted in the early 1960s described his unprecedented empirical research into Korea's legal issues. During this limited period, he conducted at least four surveys.[47] Among his early writings, even the one that adopted the traditional approach was regarded as the interdisciplinary study of law and economics.[48] His interest in the scientific method may have been growing before he stepped into the legal scholars' territory.

However, in the middle twentieth century, the empirical approach was not globally recognized as a genuine part of legal methodology. Perhaps, for this reason, Hahm clarified his article, co-authored with Seung-Doo Yang, based on their "monumental" 1963–1965 field research:

> It may be said that an empirical approach has no legitimate place in juridical science. We are well aware of the fact that law is a norm encrusted with "values" of a society. Law is said to be more than a mere factual datum. Law is by its very nature concerned with "ought." Law is a norm, if nothing else.
>
> But it is also more than a mere "ought." It is intimately concerned with the "is"; in fact, it is there to regulate the "is." A law that is a mere "ought" may be an idealistic manifesto or a beautiful slogan but it is not law. It must be effective in regulating the reality, the "is." When this "ought" gets connected with the "is," it becomes a factual datum amenable to empirical approach.[49]

Empirical legal research does not rest simply on the doctrinal analysis of positive sources of law, nor on "secondary sources,"[50] "anecdotal evidence,"[51] or "hunches"[52] for the development or evaluation of legal arguments. It requires collecting and analyzing first-hand data, designing a research structure for testing or generating a hypothesis, and, finally, constructing a quantitative or qualitative methodology.[53] This starkly contrasts with "the lack of reflection on methodological considerations"[54] characteristic of traditional legal research.

Hahm and Yang provide more than twelve pages of fairly detailed methodological descriptions, including chronologically describing each survey phase from sample design to tabulation and self-evaluation.[55] Hahm's article, published in 1969, provides a concise account:

> About a year's preparation had proceeded the actual field survey and the analysis of the results. The study was financed by a grant from the Asia Foundation. The schedule of questions used for the survey was composed after a pre-test conducted in the capital city and in a remote rural village. Out of the voting population of 12,985,015, determined on the basis of the voting list compiled by the National Election Commission for the presidential election held on October 15, 1963, 1,301 respondents were selected according to a modified form of stratified random sampling.
>
> The interviews were conducted on a nation-wide scale throughout South Korea with the chosen sample. The interviewers had been given training in advance, and they performed their task conscientiously and efficiently. The collected data were coded and tabulated by IBM machines at the Statistics Bureau of the Economic Planning Board of the Republic of Korea.[56]

Given that Korea's gross domestic product (GDP) per capita in 1963 was $104 (USD) at current prices,[57] this research was pioneering. With a national illiteracy rate of around 22%–28% in the 1960s,[58] in-person rather than mail surveys yielded a higher response rate.

This nationwide field research was designated a "legal consciousness survey."[59] The study of legal consciousness is a particular genre of empirical research developed through law and society research in the United States.[60] Critical legal studies subgroups share a burgeoning interest in studying the "legal consciousness and experiences" of cultural minority groups.[61] Korea was an ideal laboratory for empirical studies of law seeking to discover discrepancies between "law in books" and "law in action,"[62] or between "what the law *says*" and "what law *does*,"[63] because it received modern rules of law while maintaining traditional social norms. Hahm directed his attention to this "gap between the imported official law and traditional legal culture."[64]

Hahm's endeavor was undeniably monumental for first asking ordinary Koreans what they thought of Korea's laws.[65] He recognized that the "perspectives of the people" or the "cultural component of the legal process" significantly impacts the law's effectiveness.[66] Hahm achieved what he called "a small advance" toward this understanding:

> The Rule of Law is deemed essential for a workable democracy. Yet, we are saying that we must have democracy before we can have the Rule of Law. This is the vicious circle in which a developing nation such as Korea finds

> itself caught. This chain of the circle must be broken somehow. We may not expect a fast and easy formula. One thing is certain, however. If a small advance is made in one area, a similar or a greater advance may be expected in the other.[67]

The gap between official law and traditional legal culture became one of the main preoccupations of Hahm's scholarship, and it was apparently implicated in his study of legal processes and the law's effectiveness. McDougal, Lasswell, and Northrop's insightful writings provided an extra impetus for his culture-responsive and policy-oriented legal studies. Since he spent time in New Haven, scores of ideas and causes devised or championed by them resonated in his approach to legal studies; for instance, his perspective on (1) law as a policy science[68] or a process of decision;[69] (2) a grammar of symbols[70] and values;[71] (3) a depiction of power as deprivation;[72] and (4) the mediational approval theory of law.[73]

It is a tragic irony that Hahm's research on Korean legal culture was posthumously attacked by law and society scholars, who undoubtedly cherished his legacy.[74] However, a series of heated debates triggered by Kun Yang's critical review of Hahm's writings eventually contributed to legal studies in Korea. Critiques of "the Hahm theses" have evolved into methodological debates surrounding culturalism, institutionalism, and social-structuralism.[75] Economic analysis of empirical data has been integrated into the cultural study of attitudes toward litigation.[76] Hahm's preoccupation with legal culture has led to anthropologic reflections on the relationship between law and culture[77] and even reappraising his attempts to find a "unique grammar" that defines Korean legal culture.[78] These changes demonstrate that the "small advance" he achieved is no longer small. Hahm was no ordinary "black-letter man" but a "man of the future."[79]

3 Anglo-American Jurisprudential Wave

According to a legal historian, the influence of American law declined from the 1960s, and German law became more prominent in Korea's legal academia. For decades since the 1960s, most students went to Germany to study law.[80] However, the Anglo-American jurisprudential wave began surging in the late twentieth century when H.L.A. Hart's philosophy was introduced in the early 1970s.

3.1 British Jurisprudence

British legal philosophy can be roughly divided into chapters. Johannes Duns Scotus and William of Ockham's medieval legal philosophy generally established the nominalist tradition of British philosophy. The seventeenth century saw the social contract and natural rights theories of Thomas Hobbes and John Locke. William Blackstone's conservative legal philosophy and David Hume's social convention theory were presented in the eighteenth century – the "time when the modernization of law began."[81] Jeremy Bentham, John Austin, and J. S. Mill's utilitarian legal philosophies, and the liberal democratic theory of A. V. Dicey, occupied the nineteenth century. From the twentieth century onward, H.L.A. Hart's new analytical jurisprudence has been at the center of philosophical debates.

The study of British legal philosophy in Korea has, with some exceptions, focused on Hart's analytical jurisprudence and its legacy.[82] Duns Scotus and William of Ockham have not been explored beyond a conspectus of legal ideas pertaining to the medieval Scholastic School. On the other hand, several secondary writings[83] and translations of some classics from the era of Hobbes and Locke began to appear but remain little studied compared to the great German philosophers. For instance, as Hart pointed out, research has not yet been conducted on Hobbes' issue of differentiation from the perspective of the reductionist theory of law endorsed by Bentham and Austin.[84] Competing understandings – voluntarist and intellectualist approaches – regarding Locke's natural law theory and political philosophy remain for discussion.[85]

Since Hart considered the classical imperative theory of law, espoused by Bentham and Austin, an object to overcome, Korean scholars have, to that extent, become familiar with this theme. However, legal philosophers' study of Bentham remains nascent, given that Bentham as an analytical legal philosopher, not a utilitarian moralist, emerged belatedly through Hart's studies. One of the earliest writings on Bentham as a legal philosopher was published only in the 1990s.[86] In recent years, Sang-Young Lee has shown an exceptional commitment to studying the impact of Bentham's life and legal thought in Korea.[87] We can find rigorous research on Austin's theory of law in Korea, though not easily.[88] However, A. V. Dicey's constitutional ideas, including those of parliamentary supremacy and the rule of law, were introduced in detail by constitutional and administrative law scholars.[89]

We cannot discuss modern British philosophy of law without mentioning Hart's achievements. Hart, along with Hans Kelsen, is often considered one of the greatest modern philosophers of law, which is confirmed through his influence on legal philosophy at home and abroad. Before Hart, British philosophy of law did not have today's prestige. To borrow Byung-Sun Oh's observation on British and American philosophy before Hart, "political philosophy is dead and philosophy of law is about to die."[90] However, Oxford became an undisputed center for the philosophy of law for decades. Just as Hart refined his analytical legal positivism through theoretical confrontations with Patrick Devlin, Lon L. Fuller, and Ronald Dworkin, the anti-positivism that he contested renewed its theoretical approach.

A thorough study of the themes by Hart and his disciples began in Korea after the late 1970s. Hun-Sup Shim's[91] series of articles "laid the foundations on which studies of legal philosophy in Korea have come close to the world-class level."[92] Meanwhile, Hart's *Law, Liberty and Morality* and *The Concept of Law* were translated into Korean.[93]

Many sources show that contemporary British jurisprudence hugely impacted Korea's legal academia, but court decisions applying its unique traits are scant. In one of the most relevant cases, the Constitutional Court addressed the enforcement of morals.[94]

> Roads for general transportation are areas that the state and local governments are responsible for managing; they are related to the interests of other drivers, pedestrians, and the community. They cannot be evaluated in the same way as the act of enjoying dangerous sports.
>
> Considering that drivers cannot prevent the risks or damages brought about by not wearing a seatbelt from massively disadvantaging society; that even those good at driving with no seatbelt cannot diminish the risks; and that damage caused to fellow passengers would be increased, state intervention is justified because driving with the seatbelt unbuckled harms not only the drivers but the interests of the entire society.[95]

In this case, Korea's Constitutional Court attempted to develop an argument based on the harm principle, which emerged as a central tenet of liberalism during debates between J. F. Stephen and Mill, and between Devlin and Hart. The Court's decision is remarkable because, paradoxically, many decisions are silent on this liberal approach and freely stray from the harm principle.[96]

3.2 American Jurisprudence

Natural law theory provided the ideological basis for the American Revolution in the eighteenth century; after it waned in the nineteenth century, formalism and pragmatism followed. Legal formalism was represented by C. C. Langdell, who considered the law a logical system and its study a deductive science influenced by German conceptual jurisprudence. In contrast, legal pragmatism advocated by O. W. Holmes, Jr. recognized law as a means of social reform and emphasized the "utility of jurisprudence for the realization of policy" rather than conceptual scrutiny.[97] Progressive legal theory acknowledging parliamentary initiative culminated in sociological jurisprudence advanced by Roscoe Pound, who accepted Rudolph von Jhering's approach to identifying law as a means to an end. Before long, however, a new progressive movement – legal realism – emerged at Yale and Columbia in the early 1900s.[98] In the second half of the twentieth century, various academic courses such as Process Jurisprudence, Law and Society Movement, Law and Economics, and Critical Legal Studies appeared. The tradition of American legal philosophy, distinct from German and British traditions, was established.

Kyung-Hak Chang was initially overwhelmed by a bewildering array of trends in American legal studies when he attended jurisprudence seminars facilitated by Jerome Hall[99] in Bloomington, Indiana, during the 1950s.[100] Later, he described the atmosphere as "a hundred flowers bloom at once, a hundred flowers bloom all over."[101] Gyeong-Hwan Ahn and Jong-Cheol Kim evaluated American legal philosophy as "multilayered theories bolstering judicial superiority."[102]

Growing numbers of Korean legal scholars in the 1950s became interested in American law and American jurisprudence's new intellectual traditions. From 1950 to 1960, articles and books by Roscoe Pound were often translated and published in Korea.[103] Meanwhile, writings by leading legal realists of the early twentieth century were, for some reason, rarely translated. Instead, after the 1990s, Korean legal scholars continuously produced articles concerning legal realism.[104] Legal and philosophical trends in the United States that unfolded after the second half of the twentieth century are now actively studied in Korea.[105]

Under American jurisprudence's influence, Korean legal philosophers have gradually expanded their scholarly interest beyond positive sources of law to the concrete processes of judicial decision-making.[106] One of the most well-known salient features of the American tradition is the "role of the court" rather than, for instance, the "concept of law."[107] More than ever, controversial court decisions draw Korean legal philosophers' critical attention to the court's interpretive activities.

In 1994, the Korean Supreme Court decided "The Orchard on Fire" case[108] where the justices sharply divided over the interpretation of statutory language. Article 170(2) of the *Criminal Act* was revised on December 8, 2020, to read, "The preceding paragraph shall apply to a person who, through negligence, burns an object mentioned in Article 166, which is his own property, or an object mentioned in Article 167, and thereby causes public danger." The earlier version read, "The preceding paragraph shall apply to a person who, through negligence, burns an object mentioned in Article 166 or 167, which is his own property, and thereby causes public danger." The justices disagreed over reconciling these versions.

> [Majority opinion] The text of Article 170(2) of the *Criminal Act*, which reads 'an object mentioned in Article 166 or 167, which is his own property,' should be construed as 'an object mentioned in Article 166, which is his own property, or an object mentioned in Article 167 no matter whose property it is,' . . . all the related provisions considered. Since the construction does not form or create law, it is neither [an] extensive interpretation nor reasoning by analogy, which are prohibited by the principle of legality in the criminal law.

> [Dissenting opinion] The text of Article 170(2) of the *Criminal Act* does not read 'an object mentioned in Article 166, which is his own property, or an object mentioned in Article 167,' but 'an object mentioned in Article 166 or 167, which is his own property.' According to ordinary usage, the clause 'which is his own property' modifies the phrase 'an object mentioned in Article 166 or 167.' Therefore, it can be seen that the same text does not mean 'an object mentioned in Article 166, which is his own property, or an object mentioned in Article 167 *simpliciter*.'[109]

Scholars jumped into the debate surrounding the ruling. Their debate process was later summarized in a book with a preface boasting that "academic debates as such were hard to find in the legal academia of Korea."[110] Most debaters were professors in legal philosophy, along with a judge with a Ph.D. in legal philosophy. In particular, Bong-Chul Choi defended a purposivist approach against textualism in statutory construction while elaborating on the theoretical discussion in the United States.[111]

3.3 Intersection

Some of modern legal philosophy's most important debates were triggered when British and American philosophies intersected while following different paths. Each time, a novel form of anti-positivist theory emerged – Fuller's procedural theory of natural law and Dworkin's theory of principles. Through debates with Hart, these theories provided a logic – distinct from natural law theory – to confront legal positivism's separation thesis. After Dworkin's theory, legal positivism roughly divided into two camps – inclusive and exclusive legal positivism. With the Hart-Fuller and Hart-Dworkin debates, modern Anglo-American legal philosophy, including the positivist and anti-positivist camps, presented a pattern of subdivision.

Fuller and Dworkin's theories caused many repercussions in Korea. They drew public attention to issues regarding the law's morality and integrity while avoiding traditional natural law's theoretical weaknesses. Dokyun Kim asserts that Korea's Supreme Court "has changed its jurisprudence in important respects during recent periods," moving toward an interpretative goal of "taking integrity seriously."[112] Meanwhile, Fuller's *The Morality of Law* and Dworkin's *Law's Empire* were translated into Korean.[113]

Research on post-Hart analytical legal positivism is also actively conducted in Korea. In particular, interest is growing in the legal philosophy of Joseph Raz, one of legal positivism's leading exponents after Hart. Concurrently, unique keywords of Anglo-American legal philosophy, for instance authority, convention, and naturalization, are gradually being considered.

The morality of law and justice through adjudication[114] has again become a topic in a democratized Korea. For example, lawsuits against the Korean government, to regain land acquired by pro-Japanese traitors as a reward for treachery, markedly increased in the 1990s. In the early 2000s, courts in these cases attempted to bridge the gap between law and justice by elaborating a rationale for dismissing the lawsuits based on "justice" and "principle," along with positive sources of law, including the bonafide clause of the *Civil Procedure Act*[115] and the Preamble to Korea's Constitution:[116]

> It is unlawful, as it turns significantly against justice, for a person, who has chosen to renounce the independence of our nation and its self-determination and to be of service to Japanese imperialism, or his universal successor, to seek legal protection of property acquired, either directly or indirectly, via treachery by filing a lawsuit with the court as the constitutional institution, which upholds the spirit of the Constitution and its order, and is responsible, as required by the principle of the rule of law, for clearing anti-Korean

traitors. Moreover, legal stability, which is also required by the principle of the rule of law, would not be undermined if the court turned down the lawsuits.[117]

Critics objected that the court denied the traitors and their descendants justice for unclear reasons.[118] A civil procedure expert denounced the decision as an "application of the covert natural law," while contrasting it with *Riggs v. Palmer*, based on a distinction between the tolerated and the unanticipated.[119] However, the National Assembly responded with a special law[120] endorsing the political morality underlying the court's decision.[121]

4 Concluding Remarks

By accepting Anglo-American jurisprudence, scholarly interest in Korea expanded beyond positive sources of law to the concrete processes of judicial decision-making, and this change produced a variety of positive effects on Korea's legal academia. I conclude with thoughts on the direction that Korea's legal philosophy should take and the remaining issues.

First, the study of legal philosophy's relationship to public law seems quite active, but there has been insufficient research on its relationship to private law. Second, more attention should be paid to 'doing legal philosophy,' which is more important for the study and teaching of legal philosophy. It is necessary to contemplate learning and the merits of an 'interdisciplinary research climate' or 'connectedness' between legal philosophy and the other philosophical fields in American jurisprudence. Third, the participatory quality of anti-positivist legal philosophy should be enhanced. Scholars in Korea's legal academia should and can provide legal professionals, including judges, with reasonable ideas to cope with the hard cases that our society confronts. Lastly, the normative gaps between the positivist sources thesis and anti-positivist moral requirements should be considered the foundations of law. Even if there is no necessary connection between law and morality, they always evolve as a pair, and those normative gaps may be the pragmatic source of normativity.[122]

Notes

1 Joon-Young Moon, *Beob-wongwa Geomchal-ui Tansaeng [The Birth of the Court and the Prosecution]* (Seoul: Yuksabipyeongsa, 2010), 677.
2 Korean Association of Legal Philosophy, ed., *Hangug Hyeondaebeobcheolhag-ui Hyeongseong-gwa Jeongae [The Forming and Unfolding of Contemporary Legal Philosophy in Korea]* (Seoul: Sechang Publishing Company, 2010), 338.
3 Korea and Japan shared this burgeoning interest in American law during the 1950s. Makoto Oishi, "Positioning of the Problem in Japan," in *Oegugbeob-ui Gyesuwa Beoblyeong-yong-eo [Reception of Foreign Laws and Terminology in Law]*, ed. Korea Legislation Research Institute (Seoul: KLRI, 2002), 97.
4 "Purpose," translated from the abridged establishment document in 1956 provided by the Korean Society of Law (www.lawsociety.or.kr).
5 Criminal Act, Article 20.

6 Supreme Court Decision 82Do357 Decided February 8, 1983.

7 Dongwoon Shin, "Hyeongbeob Je20jo Sahoesang-gyu Gyujeong-ui Seonglib-gyeong-wi [Korean Criminal Act (Article 20)]," *Seoul Law Journal* 47, no. 2 (2006): 208 and 216.

8 Joon-Seok Park, *Beobsasang, Saeng-gaghal Uimue Daehayeo [Making Law Intelligible: Essays in Legal Ideas]*, (Seoul: Acanet, 2015), 315–16.

9 "Their allusion to the rule of law would be twofold. The first is the principle that governmental action should be based on, and circumscribed by, the legal rules. I would call it the rule of law in the narrow sense. The second implies the subjection of social life in general to legal rules. I would call it the rule of law in the broad sense." Chulwoo Lee, "Legal Culture and the Rule of Law in Korea," *Hanyang Law Review* 16 (1999): 385.

10 Pyong-Ho Pak, *Geunse-ui Beobgwa Beobsasang [Law and Legal Thoughts of Modern Ages]* (Seoul: Jinwon, 1996), 162–63.

11 Ibid., 163.

12 Paul K. Ryu and Helen Silving, "Towards a Rational System of Criminal Law," *Seoul Law Journal* 4 (1962): 11.

13 Pyong-Choon Hahm and Seung-Doo Yang, "The Attitudes of the Korean People Toward Law," in *Legal System of Korea*, ed. Shin-Yong Chun (Seoul: International Cultural Foundations, 1975), 146. This article was based on research conducted in the early 1960s. Some of the observations derived from this research were included in Hahm's article, entitled, "The Decision Process in Korea," which came out as a chapter in *Comparative Judicial Behavior: Cross-Cultural Studies of Political Decision-Making in the East and West*, eds. Clendon Schubert and David J. Danelski (New York: Oxford University Press, 1969).

14 Chongko Choi, "Ryu Kichyun-ui Yale Daehag Bagsahag-winonmun (1958) [J.S.D. Dissertation of Paul K. Ryu (1958)]," in *Korean Culture and Criminal Responsibility*, ed. Paul K. Ryu (Seoul: Bobmunsa, 2011), 327–30; Byung-Sun Oh, "Ryu Kichyun-ui Beobsasang [Legal Thoughts of Paul K. Ryu]," in *Dasi Ryu Kichyun-eul Saeng-Gaghanda* [*Rethinking Paul K. Ryu*], ed. The Paul K. Ryu Foundation (Seoul: Bobmunsa, 2015), 191–98; Young-Min Chang, "'Wolsong Ryu Kichyun Gyosuui Hyeongbeobgwan'e Daehan Tolonmun [Comment on 'Paul K. Ryu's View of Criminal Law']," in *Rethinking Paul K. Ryu*, ed. The Paul K. Ryu Foundation, 236–41 (Seoul: Bobmunsa, 2015); Chulwoo Lee, "Hahm Pyong-Choon Gyosu (1932–1983): Jeontong, Geundae, Segyeui Gyochajeom-eseo Beob-eul Malhada [Professor Pyong-Choon Hahm (1932–1983): To Speak the Law at the Intersection of Tradition, Modernity and the World]," in *Yeonsei-ui Beobhagjadeul I [Legal Scholars of Yonsei I]*, eds. Jong-Soo Lee et al. (Seoul: Yonsei University Press, 2020), 170.

15 This quote refers to Lasswell. Eugene V. Rostow, "Myres S. McDougal," *The Yale Law Journal* 84 (1975): 707.

16 Choong-Soon Kim, "Hahm Pyong-Choon Seonsaengnim-ui Salmgwa Hagmun [Dr. Pyong-Choon Hahm: His Life and Scholarship]," *Yonsei Law Review* 24, no. 2 (2014): 9.

17 Lee, "Professor Pyong-Choon Hahm (1932–1983)," 170.

18 Ryu and Silving, "Towards a Rational System of Criminal Law," 20.

19 Article 145(1) (a person, who having been in lawful arrest or custody escapes, shall be punished by imprisonment for not more than one year).

20 Paul K. Ryu, *Gaejeong Hyeongbeobhag (Chonglongang-ui) [Criminal Law: Lectures on General Provisions]*, Facsimile Edition (Seoul: Bobmunsa, 2011), 214–15.

21 Ibid., 64–65.

22 Ibid., 66–67.

23 Ibid., 64.

24 Ryu, *Korean Culture and Criminal Responsibility*, 8.
25 Stuart Chase, "Foreword," in *Language, Thought, and Reality – Selected Writings of Benjamin Lee Whorf*, ed. John B. Carroll (Cambridge: The Technology Press of MIT, 1956), v. Ryu quoted this phrase in his J.S.D. dissertation. Ryu, *Korean Culture and Criminal Responsibility.*
26 Chun-Soo Yang, "Sangjingjuui Hyeongbeob-ilon: Ryu Kichyun Gyosuui Hyeongbeobcheolhag [The Theory of Symbolic Criminal Law: Paul K. Ryu's Philosophy of Criminal Law]," *Korean Journal of Law & Society* 64 (2020): 108.
27 Ryu, *Criminal Law*, 67.
28 Ryu, *Korean Culture and Criminal Responsibility*, 38.
29 Paul K. Ryu and Helen Silving, "Was bedeutet die sogenannte 'Relativität der Rechtsbegriffe'?" *ARSP* 59, no. 1 (1973): 57–86; Yang, "The Theory of Symbolic Criminal Law," 105 note 5, 123, and 133–35.
30 Ryu, *Criminal Law*, xii ("Foreword" of the first edition in 1960).
31 Ryu, *Korean Culture and Criminal Responsibility*, 148, 155, and 165.
32 Ibid., 145–81.
33 Ryu and Silving, "Towards a Rational System of Criminal Law," 18.
34 Chongko Choi, "Ryu Kichyun-ui Beobsasang [Legal Thoughts of Paul Kichyon Ryu]," *Seoul Law Journal* 40, no. 1 (1999): 183–84.
35 Chang, "Comment," 232.
36 Ryu, *Criminal Law*, 138.
37 Ryu and Silving, "Towards a Rational System of Criminal Law," 23–24.
38 Chang, "Comment," 233.
39 Paul K. Ryu, "Causation in Criminal Law," *University of Pennsylvania Law Review* 106, no. 6 (1958): 156; Ryu, *Criminal Law*, 150–53.
40 Ryu, *Criminal Law*, 137–40.
41 Chang, "Comment," 236, 241–42.
42 Ryu, *Korean Culture and Criminal Responsibility*, 4.
43 The Paul K. Ryu Foundation, *Rethinking Paul K. Ryu*, 75.
44 Paul K. Ryu, "Beobgwa Pyeonghwa [Law and Peace]," in *Jayusahoeui Beobgwa Jeong-ui [Law and Justice in a Free Society]*, ed. The Paul K. Ryu Foundation (Seoul: Bobmunsa, 2015), 94.
45 Ryu, *Korean Culture and Criminal Responsibility*, 181.
46 He had majored in economics as an undergraduate at Northwestern University prior to Harvard Law School, class of 1959.
47 They each provided the source for the following articles: (a) Pyong-Choon Hahm, "Beob-ui Silhyoseong-gwa Gongmuwon [Efficacy of Law and Public Officials]," *Journal of Law and Administration* 4 (1963): 123–229; Pyong-Choon Hahm, "The Korean People and Their Property Rights," *The American Journal of Comparative Law* 12, no. 1 (1963): 61–71; (b) Pyong-Choon Hahm, Choong-Soon Kim, and Seung-Doo Yang, "Hangug Nodongjohab-ui Hyeonsilgwa Nodongbeob [Labor Law and the Reality of the Trade Unionism in Korea]," *Yonsei Nonchong* 3, no. 1 (1964): 213–250; (c) Pyong-Choon Hahm and Byong-Je Jon, "The Criminality of Abortion in Korea," *Journal of Criminal Law and Criminology* 56, no. 1 (1965): 18–26; and (d) Pyong-Choon Hahm, "The Decision Process in Korea," and Pyong-Choon Hahm and Seung-Doo Yang, "The Attitudes of the Korean People Toward Law." Another article entitled "A Study on the Korean Preference for Male Children" was written around the 1970s and is based on in-depth interviews, but it is not known exactly when the interviews were conducted. This article was reprinted in *Korean Jurisprudence, Politics and Culture*, ed. Pyong-Choon Hahm (Seoul: Yonsei University Press, 1986), 213–40.
48 Pyong-Choon Hahm, "Beob-ui Gineung-gwa Gyeongjesaenghwal [The Function of Law and the Economic Life]," *Yonsei Nonchong* 1 (1962): 145–77.

49 Hahm and Yang, "The Attitudes of the Korean People Toward Law," 145.
50 John Baldwin and Gwynn Davis, "Empirical Research in Law," in *The Oxford Handbook of Legal Studies*, eds. Peter Cane and Mark Tushnet (Oxford: Oxford University Press, 2003), 880–81.
51 Michael Heise, "The Importance of Being Empirical," *Pepperdine Law Review* 26 (1999): 808.
52 Tom R. Tyler, "Methodology in Legal Research," *Utrecht Law Review* 13, no. 3 (2017): 131.
53 Michael Adler and Jonathan Simon, "Stepwise Progression: The Past, Present, and Possible Future of Empirical Research on Law in the United States and the United Kingdom," *Journal of Law and Society* 41, no. 2 (2014): 176.
54 Philip Langbroek et al., "Methodology of Legal Research: Challenges and Opportunities," *Utrecht La Review* 13, no. 3 (2017): 2.
55 Hahm and Yang, "The Attitudes of the Korean People Toward Law," 146–57.
56 Pyong-Choon Hahm, "The Decision Process in Korea," note 12. This article was reprinted in *Korean Jurisprudence, Politics and Culture*, Pyong-Choon Hahm, 95–121, and the quote is at 97.
57 "Gross Domestic Product per Capita (Current Prices) 1960–2020," Statistical Database at Korean Statistical Information Service (KOSIS), accessed April 13, 2022, https://kosis.kr/statHtml/statHtml.do?orgId=101&tblId=DT_2KAA902&vw_cd=MT_RTITLE&list_id=101_003_L&scrId=&seqNo=&lang_mode=ko&obj_var_id=&itm_id=&conn_path=MT_RTITLE&path=%252FstatisticsList%252FstatisticsListIndex.do.
58 Jinhee Kim et al., *EFA National Report: Republic of Korea* (Seoul: Korean National Commission for UNESCO, 2014), 32.
59 According to a sociologist of law, "in Korea, the research of legal consciousness has been regarded as a synonym for law and society studies." Kun Yang, "Hangugeseoui 'Beobgwa Sahoe' Yeongu [The 'Law and Society' Studies in Korea]," *Korean Journal of Law & Society* 1 (1989): 68. Meanwhile, a social anthropologist relates Hahm's research to legal anthropology rather than law and society studies. Choong-Soon Kim, "Dr. Pyong-Choon Hahm: His Life and Scholarship," 9.
60 Susan Silbey, "After Legal Consciousness," *Annual Review of Law and Social Science* 1 (2005): 324 and 335.
61 Adler and Simon, "Stepwise Progression," 181.
62 Roscoe Pound, "Law in Books and Law in Action," *American Law Review* 44 (1910): 12.
63 Baldwin and Davis, "Empirical Research in Law," 881 [emphasis included].
64 Lee, "Editor's Note," 115.
65 Kim, "Dr. Pyong-Choon Hahm: His Life and Scholarship," 8.
66 Pyong-Choon Hahm, "The Traditional Patterns of Authoritative Symbols and the Judicial Process in Korea," in *Korean Jurisprudence, Politics and Culture*, ed. Pyong-Choon Hahm (Seoul: Yonsei University Press, 1986), 4.
67 Pyong-Choon Hahm, "The Rule of What Law? A Korean Conundrum," *Journal of the International Commission of Jurists* 6, no. 2 (1965): 284 [footnote omitted]. The same text can also be found at *id.*, *The Korean Political Tradition and Law: Essays in Korean Law and Legal History*, 2nd ed. (Seoul: Hollym Corporation, 1971), 214.
68 Pyong-Choon Hahm, "Law and International Education Exchange: Vocational Training or Policy Science?," *International Education: Link for Human Understanding* (keynote speech at conference), Georgia State University, 1976. Reprinted in *Korean Jurisprudence, Politics and Culture*, Pyong-Choon Hahm, 524–28 (see 527–28).
69 Hahm, "The Traditional Patterns," 8; Hahm *id.*, "The Decision Process in Korea," 95–97. This article was reprinted in *Korean Jurisprudence, Politics and Culture*, *id.* [references are to the reprint].

70 Hahm, "The Traditional Patterns," 6.

71 Pyong-Choon Hahm, "The Affective Society: Values and Law in Korea," in *Values and Development: Appraising Asian Experience*, eds. H. D. Lasswell et al. (Cambridge: The MIT Press, 1976), 190–232. Reprinted in *Korean Jurisprudence, Politics and Culture*, Pyong-Choon Hahm, 282–317 (see 282).

72 Pyong-Choon Hahm, "The Decision Process in Korea," 97; Pyong-Choon Hahm *id.*, "Toward a New Theory of Korean Politics: A Reexamination of Traditional Factors," in *Korean Politics in Transition*, ed. Edward R. Wright ed. (Seattle: University of Washington Press, 1975), 321–356. Reprinted in *Korean Jurisprudence, Politics and Culture*, Pyong-Choon Hahm, 252–281 (see 275).

73 Hahm, "The Decision Process in Korea," 96.

74 Kun Yang, "The Law and Society Studies in Korea: Beyond the Hahm Theses," *Law & Society Review* 23, no. 5 (1989): 894–98; Chulwoo Lee, "Talking about Korean Legal Culture: A Critical Review of the Discursive Production of Legal Culture in Korea," *Korea Journal* 38, no. 3 (1998): 53–69; Sahng-Hyeog Ihm, "Sosong Gipiui Munhwajeontong-e Daehan Jaegowa Hangugsahoe [Lawsuit Avoiding Tradition in East Asia and Reconsideration of It in Korean Society]," *Korean Journal of Law & Society* 25 (2003): 151–57.

75 Chulwoo Lee, "Beobmunhwaui Damlonjeog Saengsan: Bangbeoblonjeog Bipan [The Discursive Production of Legal Culture: A Methodological Critique]," *Korean Journal of Legal Philosophy* 14, no. 1 (2001): 203–30.

76 Du-Eol Kim, *Gyeongjeseongjang-gwa Sabeobjeongchaeg [Economic Growth and Judicial Policy]* (Seoul: Haenam Publishing, 2011) (see Chapter 2).

77 Jeong-Oh Kim, "Simin-ui Beobmunhwa (I): Beobmunhwaui Saeloun Insig [Citizens' Legal Culture (I): The New Perspective of Law and Culture]," *Yonsei Law Review* 8 (1998): 149–94.

78 Jeong-Oh Kim, "Hahm Pyong-Choon Seonsaeng-ui Hangugbeobmunhwalon [Dr. Hahm Pyong-Choon's Thought on Korean Legal Culture]," *Yonsei Law Review* 24, no. 2 (2014): 55.

79 O. W. Holmes, Jr., "The Path of the Law," *Harvard Law Review* 10 (1897): 457 ff. Reprinted in *Harvard Law Review* 110, no. 5 (1997): 991–1009 (see 1001).

80 Chongko Choi, *Hangugbeobhagsa [A History of Korean Legal Theory]* (Seoul: Pakyoungsa, 1990), 473.

81 Gyong-Whan Ahn and Jong-Cheol Kim, "Yeong-gugbeobgwa Migugbeob-ui Bigyo Yeongu (V) – Beob-ilon (1) [Comparative Analysis of Anglo-American Law (V) – Legal Theories (1)]," *Seoul Law Journal* 40, no. 1 (1999): 218.

82 One of the earliest writings on Hart's legal positivism was published no later than the late 1960s. Uon-Bae Tjon, "Agbeob-ui Beobli – Agbeobgyujun-e Iss-eoseoui Beobsiljeungjuuiwa Beob-uisig-ui Gineung [On the Principle of Evil Law]," *Seoul Law Journal* 11, no. 1 (1969): 5–34.

83 Il-Kyung Park, "Hobbes-wa Locke-e Iss-eoseoui Ingwon [Human Rights in Hobbes and Locke]," *Bubjo* 17, no. 8 (1968): 1–12; Zai-Woo Shim, "Thomas Hobbes-ui Beobsasang [Legal Thought of Thomas Hobbes]," in *Beobsasang-gwa Minsabeob [Legal Thought and Civil Law: Festschrift for Dr. Seung-Jong Hyeon]*, ed. Publication Committee (Seoul: Kookminbooks Co., Ltd., 1979), 61–83; Un-Jong Pak, "Gihahag-ui Jeongsingwa Geundaejayeonbeob [The Spirit of Geometry and the Modern Law of Nature]," *Ewha Journal of Social Sciences* 6 (1986): 3–14 and Un-Jong Pak, "Bangbeobsajeog Gwanjeom-eseo Bon Hobbes-ui Jayeonbeobsasang [Thomas Hobbes' Thinking about Natural Law – Methodological Consideration]," *Korea Cultural Research Institute Nonchong* 49 (1986): 363–80; Tai-Uk Chung, "Geundae Soyugwonsasang-ui Hyeongseong – Yeong-gug-ui Gyeong-uleul Jungsim-eulo [An Analysis of the Development of the Modern Conception of Property Rights]," *Korean Journal of Legal Philosophy* 3, no. 1 (2000): 63–88; Dong-Ryong Shin, "Jayujuuijeog Jeojaggwon Damlon-ui Seong-gwawa Hangyee Daehan Gochal [The Contributions and Limits of the Liberal Copyright Theory]," *Korean Journal*

of Legal Philosophy 8, no. 1 (2005): 113–50; Zai-Wang Yoon, "Gaeinjuuijeog Jeoldaejuui – Thomas Hobbes-ui Guggacheolhaggwa Beobcheolhag-e Gwanhayeo [Individualistic Absolutism: About the Philosophy of Law and State of Thomas Hobbes]," *Journal of Law Research* 28, no. 2 (2012): 7–36.

84 H.L.A. Hart, *Essays on Bentham: Studies in Jurisprudence and Political Theory* (Oxford: Clarendon Press, 1982), 253.

85 Korean Association of Legal Philosophy, *The Forming and Unfolding of Contemporary Legal Philosophy in Korea*, 345 note 37.

86 Gyong-Whan Ahn and Jong-Cheol Kim, "Bentham, Modernity and the Nineteenth Century Revolution in Government," *Seoul Law Journal* 35, no. 3 & 4 (1994): 135–55.

87 Sang-Young Lee, "Bentham-ui Beobgaenyeomgwa Ibbeoblon-e Daehan Sogo [The Study on the Concept of Law and the Theory Legislation]," *World Constitutional Law Review* 13, no. 2 (2007): 149–94; Sang-Young Lee, "Bentham-ui Common Law Chegyee Daehan Bipangwa Ibbeoblon Gusang-e Daehan Yeongu [A Search for New Perspectives on Judicial Precedent: A Study about the Criticism on the Common Law System and the Construction of Theory of Legislation]," *Seoul Law Journal* 49, no. 3 (2008): 1–39; Sang-Young Lee, "Gonglijuui Dae Jayeongwon [Theory of Utilitarianism versus Natural Rights]," *World Constitutional Law Review* 16, no. 2 (2010): 295–334; Sang-Young Lee, "Sabeob Dae Ibbeob – Bentham-ui 'Pannomion (Wanjeonhan Beobchegye)'e Daehan Yeongu ['Adjudication' versus 'Legislation' – Under J. Bentham's 'Pannomion']," *Ilkam Law Review* 21 (2012): 557–612; Sang-Young Lee, "J. Bentham-ui Segyeheonbeob Gusang-e Daehan Sogo – Segye Gongtong Heonbeob? [A Study on Bentham's Conception of the Constitutional Law of the World – A Common Constitutional Law?]," *Ajou Law Research* 8, no. 3 (2014): 145–78; Sang-Young Lee, "Gonglijuuijaui Heonbeobjeon Yeongu – J. Bentham-ui 'Heonbeobjeon'ui Guseong-gwa Teugjing [A Study on the Utilitarian Constitutional Code – Aspects and Figures of Bentham's 'Constitutional Code']," *Inha Law Review* 19, no. 3 (2016): 213–51; Sang-Young Lee, "J. Bentham 'Heonbeobjeon'eseoui Ibbeobbue Daehan Yeongu: 'Segyegongtongheonbeob'eseoui Ibbeobbuui Gineung, Gwonhan, Geuligo Guseong-eun Eotteohge Doel Geos-inga [A Study on the Legislature in Bentham's Constitutional Code: Power, Function, and Structure of the Legislature in Bentham's Constitutional Code]," *Legislation and Policy Studies* 8, no. 2 (2016): 167–92.

88 Kwang-Seo Park, "Siljeungjuuibeobhag-ui Seongu (J. Austin) [A Precursor of Legal Positivism (J. Austin)]," in *Geundaebeobsasang-ui Jeongae [The Unfolding of Modern Legal Thought: Festschrift for Dr. Gyung-Hak Chang]*, ed. Publication Committee (Seoul: Shinheung Printing Co., Ltd., 1977), 105–17; Kuk-Woon Lee, "19-segi Yeong-gug-ui Bunseogbeobhag – John Austin-ui Beob-ilon-eul Jungsim-eulo [Analytical Jurisprudence in 19th Century Britain]," *Korean Journal of Legal Philosophy* 3, no. 2 (2000): 35–64; Kyung-Hwi Kwon and Jeong-Oh Kim, "John Austin-ui Saeng-aewa Beobsasang [John Austin's Life and His Legal Thought]," *Korean Journal of Legal Philosophy* 21, no. 3 (2018): 89–128; Hyung-Suk Kim, "Siljeungjuuiwa Gonglijuuiui Yeongyeol Goli – John Austin-ui Myeonglyeong-euloseoui Beob Gaenyeom [The Connection between Utilitarianism and Positivism – John Austin's Conception of Positive Law as Command]," *Hanyang Law Review* 36, no. 4 (2019): 451–92.

89 Se-Chang Yoon, "Beob-ui Jibaeui Beobli (A.V. Dicey) [Principle of the Rule of Law (A.V. Dicey)]," in *The Unfolding of Modern Legal Thought*, ed. Publication Committee (Seoul: Shinheung Printing Co., Ltd., 1977), 118–34; A. V. Dicey, *Introduction to the Study of the Law of the Constitution*, trans. Gyong-Whan Ahn and Jong-Cheol Kim (Seoul: Kyongsaewon, 1993); Jong-Cheol Kim, "Dicey-ui Beobsasang-gwa Jeongchisasang – Geu Sanghogwanlyeonseong-e Jumoghayeo [The Legal Theory and Political Ideal of Albert Venn Dicey – with Special Reference to Their Relationship]," *Korean Journal of Legal Philosophy* 7, no. 2 (2004): 39–62.

90 Byung-Sun Oh, "Hart-ui Beobcheolhag Bangbeobgwa Beob-ui Gaenyeom [H.L.A. Hart's Method of Jurisprudence and the Concept of Law]," in *Hyeondaebeobcheolhag-ui Heuleum [The Current of Legal Philosophy]*, ed. Korean Association of Legal Philosophy (Seoul: Bobmunsa, 1996), 21.

91 Hun-Sup Shim, "Beobgwa Dodeog-ui Gwangye [On the Relationship between Law and Morals]," *Seoul Law Journal* 18, no. 1 (1977): 226–36; Hun-sup Shim, "Bipanjeog Beobsiljeungjuui [Critical Legal Positivism]," in *Hyeondaesahoegwahagbangbeoblon [Methods of Modern Social Science]*, ed. Korea Social Science Institute (Seoul: Minumsa, 1977), 151–69; Hun-sup Shim, "H.L.A. Hart-ui Bunseogjeog Beob-ilon [H.L.A. Hart's Analytical Jurisprudence]," *Sabeob-Haengjeong* 19, no. 3 (1978): 48–54; Hun-Sup Shim, "Beob-ui Hyolyeog-e Gwanhan Yeongu [Investigations into the Validity of the Law]," *Seoul Law Journal* 21, no. 1 (1980): 141–73; Hun-sup Shim, "Beobgaenyeom-e Gwanhan Non-ui [Discussions on the Concept of Law]," *Seoul Law Journal* 31, no. 1 & 2 (1990): 61–72; Hun-sup Shim, "Gwon-wie Gwanhayeo – Baejejeog Beobsiljeungjuuieseo Poyongjeog Beobsiljeungjuuielo [About Authority]," *Seoul Law Journal* 39, no. 2 (1998): 103–23.

92 Dokyun Kim, "Seouldaehaggyo Beobhag 50-nyeon-eul Doedol-abomyeo: Beobcheolhag Bun-ya [Looking Back on 50 years of the *Seoul Law Journal* – Philosophy of Law]," *Seoul Law Journal* 50, no. 2 (2009): 77.

93 H.L.A. Hart, *Law, Liberty and Morality*, trans. Young-Rahn Lee (Seoul: Nanam, 1996); H.L.A. Hart, *The Concept of Law*, trans. Byung-Sun Oh, 2nd ed. (Seoul: Acanet, 2001).

94 Bong-Chul Choi, *Hyeondaebeobcheolhag – Yeong-eogwon Beobcheolhag-eul Jungsim-eulo [Modern Legal Philosophy: Focusing on Legal Philosophy of the English-Speaking World]* (Seoul: Bobmunsa, 2007), 369–405.

95 Constitutional Court Decision 2002Hun-Ma518 Decided October 30, 2003.

96 Dokyun Kim, "Beob-wonliloseoui Gong-ig – Jayugonghwajuui Gong-iggwan-ui Sigag-eseo [Public Interest as a Legal Principle: A Liberal-Republican Conception of the Public Interest]," *Seoul Law Journal* 47, no. 3 (2006): 197–208; Choi, *Modern Legal Philosophy*, 396–405; Park, *Making Law Intelligible*, 28–38.

97 Gyong-Whan Ahn and Jong-Cheol Kim, "Yeong-gugbeobgwa Migugbeob-ui Bigyo Yeongu (V) – Beob-ilon (2) [Comparative Analysis of Anglo-American Law (V) – Legal Theories (2)]," *Seoul Law Journal* 40, no. 2 (1999): 165–66.

98 Ahn and Kim, "Comparative Analysis of Anglo-American Law (V) – Legal Theories (2)," 166–68. Roscoe Pound was often considered "one of the earliest legal realists." Adler and Simon, "Stepwise Progression," 178.

99 "Asked by the U.S. Department of State to assist in the reconstruction of Korea's legal system in 1954, Hall was later named honorary director of the Korean Legal Institute . . ." (Jerome Hall Law Library, Indiana University, accessed April 13, 2022, https://law.indiana.edu/lawlibrary/about/jerome-hall.html).

100 Chongko Choi, *Hangugbeobsasangsa [A History of Korean Legal Thought]* (Seoul: Seoul National University Press, 1989), 360.

101 Kyung-Hak Chang, "Migugbeoblyulhag-ui Je Gyeonghyang [Trends in American Jurisprudence]," *Justice* 17, no. 9 (1968): 5. He was interested in the law and society Movement and legal realism. He wrote several articles on those trends and translated Jerome Hall's *Living Law of Democratic Society* and Oliver W. Holmes Jr.'s *The Common Law*. Kyung-Hak Chang, "Migugbeob-e Iss-eoseo Hyeonsiljuuiui Beob-ilon (1) [Legal Realists in the American Law (1)]," *Bubjo* 7, no. 9 (1958): 23–41; Kyung-Hak Chang, "Migugbeob-e Iss-eoseo Hyeonsiljuuiui Beob-ilon (2) [Legal Realists in the American Law (2)]," *Bubjo* 7, no. 10 (1958): 21–32; Jerome Hall, *Living Law of Democratic Society*, trans. Jerome Hall (Seoul: Eulyoo Publishing Co., 1960); Oliver W. Holmes Jr., *The Common Law*, trans. Oliver W. Holmes (Seoul: Sudomunhwasa, 1962).

102 Ahn and Kim, "Comparative Analysis of Anglo-American Law (V) – Legal Theories (2)," 152.

103 In addition to a few articles by Roscoe Pound, his books included, *The Spirit of the Common Law*, trans. Chung-Han Kim (Seoul: Minjungseogwan, 1950); Roscoe Pound, *The Task of Law*, trans. Hyo-Young Kim and Ih-Jun Ahn (Seoul: Wiseongmunhwasa, 1955); Roscoe Pound, *Interpretations of Legal History*, trans. Byeong-Guk Go (Seoul: Ilhan Publishing Co., 1956); Roscoe Pound, *New Paths of the Law*, trans. Byeong-Guk Go and Bum-Chan Lee (Seoul: Bobmunsa, 1958); Roscoe Pound, *Justice According to Law*, trans. Ton-Kak Suh (Seoul: Bobmunsa, 1959); Roscoe Pound, *An Introduction to the Philosophy of Law*, trans. Hang-Neyong Yi and Yeo-Su Kim (Seoul: Jungumsa, 1960).

104 Bong-Chul Choi, "Beobhyeonsiljuuiui Ihaeleul Wihayeo [For the Understanding of Legal Realism]," in *The Current of Legal Philosophy*, ed. Korean Association of Legal Philosophy (Seoul: Bobmunsa, 1996), 215–39; Bong-Chul Choi, "Beobhyeonsiljuui [Legal Realism]," *American Studies* 20 (1997): 1–40; Gi Young Cho, "Migug-ui Beobhyeonsiljuui Nonjaeng-e Gwanhan Gochal [A Study of American Legal Realism – Pound-Llewellyn Debate]," *Korean Journal of Legal Philosophy* 10, no. 1 (2007): 281–314; Kye Il Lee, "'Silje Sog-ui Beob' Gwannyeom-eul Jungsim-eulo Bon Hyeonsiljuui Beob-ilon-ui Byeoncheon [Transformation of Realistic Legal Theory: Focus on the Conception of 'Law in Action']," *Yonsei Law Review* 20, no. 1 (2010): 146–87.

105 Kun Yang, "Migug Beobsasang-eseoui Geubjinjuuijeog Heuleum [Radical Trends in American Legal Thought]," *American Studies* 8 (1985): 1–12; Jeong-Oh Kim, "Migug Bipanbeobhag-ui Heuleumgwa Donghyang" [Trends of Critical Legal Studies in the US]," *Korean Journal of Law & Society* 10 (1994): 239–63; Jeong-Oh Kim, "Jayujuui Beobchegyee Daehan Gujojeog Bunseoggwa Bipan – Deonkeon Kenediui Bipanbeobdamlon-eul Jungsim-eulo [Structural Analysis and Criticism of the Liberal Legal System]," *Yonsei Law Journal* 2 (1992): 653–82; Jeong-Oh Kim, "Bipanbeobhag-ui Woncheongwa Jaengjeomdeul [Sources and Issues of Critical Legal Studies]," in *The Current of Legal Philosophy*, ed. Korean Association of Legal Philosophy (Seoul: Bobmunsa, 1996), 240–70; Un-Jong Pak, "Yeoseongjuuiwa Bipanjeog Beob-ilon [Feminism and Critical Legal Theory]," in Korean Association of Legal Philosophy ed., *The Current of Legal Philosophy* (Seoul: Bobmunsa, 1996), 271–322; Jeong-Oh Kim, "Roberto Unger-ui Sahoeilongwa Beob-ilon [Roberto Unger's Social Theory and Legal Theory]," *HUFS Law Review* 27 (2007): 615–51.

106 Un-Jong Pak, "Beobhaeseogbangbeob-eseo Bon Heonbeob Je-103-jo Beobgwan-ui Doglibgwa Yangsim [The Independence and Conscience of Judges Based on the Interpretive Method for Article 103 of the Korean Constitution]," *Seoul Law Journal* 57, no. 2 (2016): 63–103.

107 Ahn and Kim, "Comparative Analysis of Anglo-American Law (V) – Legal Theories (2)," 161; Un-Jong Pak, "Beobgwangwa Beobcheolhag [The Judge and Legal Philosophy]," *Seoul Law Journal* 53, no. 1 (2012): 304.

108 It has nothing to do with Shena Mackay's novel of the same title.

109 Supreme Court en banc Decision 94Mo32 Decided December 20, 1994. The orchard, which burned to the ground from an accidental fire, belonged to "an object mentioned in Article 167 which is *not* the property of the accused." The accused would be punishable under Article 170(2) according to the majority opinion but not the dissenting opinion.

110 Dongwoon Shin et al., *Beoblyulhaeseog-ui Hangye [The Limit of Statutory Interpretation]* (Seoul: Bobmunsa, 2000), iii.

111 Bong-Chul Choi, "Mun-eonjungsimjeog Beobhaeseoglon Bipan [A Critique of the Traditional Semantic Model of Legal Interpretation]," in *The Limit of Statutory Interpretation*, eds. Dongwoon Shin et al. (Seoul: Bobmunsa, 2000), 149–78. Recently, he detailed his idea on this issue. Bong-Chul Choi, "Migug-ui

Beoblyulhaeseoglon Gaegwan [The Methodologies of Statutory Interpretation in the US]," *Justice* 176 (2020): 204–36.

112 Dokyun Kim, "Uli Daebeob-won Beobhaeseoglon-ui Jeonhwan: Ronald Dworkin-ui Nun-eulo Ilg-gi – Beob-ui Tong-ilseong-eul Hyanghayeo [Taking Integrity Seriously: Recent Trends in the Jurisprudence of the Korean Supreme Court]," *Korean Journal of Legal Philosophy* 13, no. 1 (2010): 138.

113 Lon L. Fuller, *The Morality of Law*, trans. Gu Jin Kang (Seoul: Bobmunsa, 1971); Ronald Dworkin, *Law's Empire*, trans. Young-Min Chang (Seoul: Acanet, 2004). After the translation of *Law's Empire*, most of Dworkin's major works were translated into Korean.

114 Young-Whan Kim, *Beobcheolhag-ui Geunbonmunje [Fundamental Issues of Legal Philosophy]* (Seoul: Hongmoonsa, 2012), 24.

115 Article 1(2) (the parties concerned and participants in litigation shall perform the litigation in good faith).

116 It reads, "We, the people of Korea, proud of a resplendent history and traditions dating from time immemorial, upholding the cause of the Provisional Republic of Korea Government born of the March First Independence Movement of 1919. . . ."

117 Seoul District Court Decision 99Gahap30782 Decided January 16, 2001.

118 Kim, *Fundamental Issues of Legal Philosophy*, 26–27.

119 Choong-Soo Han, "Sin-uichig-e Gihan Sogwon-ui Bagtalgwa Jeongjiui Jeongdangseong Yeobue Gwanhayeo [Deprivation and Suspension of the Right of Action on the Basis of the Principle of Good Faith]," *Hanyang Law Review* 23, no. 1 (2006): 15–17.

120 The Special Act on Asset Confiscation for Pro-Japanese and Anti-national Collaborators to the State (2005).

121 Sun-Hee Lee, the judge at the time, said, "I think the court decision occasioned the National Assembly to enact the special law on confiscating the property of pro-Japanese traitors. I thought it would be against justice to pass the property they received, in return for actively cooperating in taking our country and destroying it[,] down to their descendants." Interview with Seoul Bar Association Bulletin, November 29, 2018, http://news.seoulbar.or.kr/news/articleView.html?idxno=1302.

122 Chueh-An Yen, "Normative Gap, Subjugation and Recognition," *Proceedings of the XXII World Congress of Philosophy* 40 (2008): 185–94.

Bibliography

Adler, Michael, and Jonathan Simon. "Stepwise Progression: The Past, Present, and Possible Future of Empirical Research on Law in the United States and the United Kingdom." *Journal of Law and Society* 41, no. 2 (2014): 173–202.

Ahn, Gyong-Whan, and Jong-Cheol Kim. "Bentham, Modernity and the Nineteenth Century Revolution in Government." *Seoul Law Journal* 35, no. 3 & 4 (1994): 135–55.

———. "Yeong-gugbeobgwa Migugbeob-ui Bigyo Yeongu (V) – Beob-ilon (1) [Comparative Analysis of Anglo-American Law (V) – Legal Theories (1)]." *Seoul Law Journal* 40, no. 1 (1999): 211–40.

———. "Yeong-gugbeobgwa Migugbeob-ui Bigyo Yeongu (V) – Beob-ilon (2) [Comparative Analysis of Anglo-American Law (V) – Legal Theories (2)]." *Seoul Law Journal* 40, no. 2 (1999): 152–81.

Baldwin, John, and Gwynn Davis. "Empirical Research in Law." In *The Oxford Handbook of Legal Studies*, edited by Peter Cane and Mark Tushnet, 880–900. Oxford: Oxford University Press, 2003.

Chang, Kyung-Hak. "Migugbeob-e Iss-eoseo Hyeonsiljuuiui Beob-ilon (1) [Legal Realists in the American Law (1)]." *Bubjo* 7, no. 9 (1958): 23–41.
———. "Migugbeob-e Iss-eoseo Hyeonsiljuuiui Beob-ilon (2) [Legal Realists in the American Law (2)]." *Bubjo* 7, no. 10 (1958): 21–32.
———. "Migugbeoblyulhag-ui Je Gyeonghyang [Trends in American Jurisprudence]." *Justice* 17, no. 9 (1968): 5–9.
Chang, Young-Min. " 'Wolsong Ryu Kichyun Gyosuui Hyeongbeobgwan'e Daehan Tolonmun [Comment on 'Paul K. Ryu's View of Criminal Law']." In *Dasi Ryu Kichyun-eul Saeng-Gaghanda [Rethinking Paul K. Ryu]*, edited by The Paul K. Ryu Foundation, 231–42. Seoul: Bobmunsa, 2015.
Cho, Gi Young. "Migug-ui Beobhyeonsiljuui Nonjaeng-e Gwanhan Gochal [A Study of American Legal Realism – Pound-Llewellyn Debate]." *Korean Journal of Legal Philosophy* 10, no. 1 (2007): 281–314.
Choi, Bong-Chul. "Beobhyeonsiljuuiui Ihaeleul Wihayeo [For the Understanding of Legal Realism]." In *Hyeondaebeobcheolhag-ui Heuleum [The Current of Legal Philosophy]*, edited by Korean Association of Legal Philosophy, 215–39. Seoul: Bobmunsa, 1996.
———. "Beobhyeonsiljuui [Legal Realism]." *American Studies* 20 (1997): 1–40.
———. "Mun-eonjungsimjeog Beobhaeseoglon Bipan [A Critique of the Traditional Semantic Model of Legal Interpretation]." In *Beoblyulhaeseog-ui Hangye [The Limit of Statutory Interpretation]*, edited by Dongwoon Shin et al., 149–78. Seoul: Bobmunsa, 2000.
———. *Hyeondaebeobcheolhag – Yeong-eogwon Beobcheolhag-eul Jungsim-eulo [Modern Legal Philosophy: Focusing on Legal Philosophy of the English-Speaking World]*. Seoul: Bobmunsa, 2007.
———. "Migug-ui Beoblyulhaeseoglon Gaegwan [The Methodologies of Statutory Interpretation in the US]." *Justice* 176 (2020): 204–36.
Choi, Chongko. *Hangugbeobsasangsa [A History of Korean Legal Thought]*. Seoul: Seoul National University Press, 1989.
———. *Hangugbeobhagsa [A History of Korean Legal Theory]*. Seoul: Pakyoungsa, 1990.
———. "Ryu Kichyun-ui Beobsasang [Legal Thoughts of Paul Kichyon Ryu]." *Seoul Law Journal* 40, no. 1 (1999): 176–210.
———. *East Asian Jurisprudence*. Seoul: Seoul National University Press, 2009.
———. "Ryu Kichyun-ui Yale Daehag Bagsahag-winonmun (1958) [J.S.D. Dissertation of Paul K. Ryu (1958)]." In *Korean Culture and Criminal Responsibility*, Paul K. Ryu, 327–41. Seoul: Bobmunsa, 2011.
Chung, Tai-Uk. "Geundae Soyugwonsasang-ui Hyeongseong – Yeong-gug-ui Gyeong-uleul Jungsim-eulo [An Analysis of the Development of the Modern Conception of Property Rights]." *Korean Journal of Legal Philosophy* 3, no. 1 (2000): 63–88.
Dicey, A. V. *Introduction to the Study of the Law of the Constitution*. Translated by Gyong-Whan Ahn and Jong-Cheol Kim. Seoul: Kyongsaewon, 1993.
Dworkin, Ronald. *Law's Empire*. Translated by Young-Min Chang. Seoul: Acanet, 2004.
Fuller, Lon L. *The Morality of Law*. Translated by Gu Jin Kang. Seoul: Bobmunsa, 1971.
Hahm, Chai-Bong. "Asiajeog Gachiwa Minjujuui [Asian Values and Democracy]." *Journal of the Society of Philosophical Studies* 44 (1999): 17–33.

Hahm, Pyong-Choon. "Beob-ui Gineung-gwa Gyeongjesaenghwal [The Function of Law and the Economic Life]." *Yonsei Nonchong* 1 (1962): 145–77.

———. "Beob-ui Silhyoseong-gwa Gongmuwon [Efficacy of Law and Public Officials]." *Journal of Law and Administration* 4 (1963): 123–229.

———. "The Korean People and Their Property Rights." *The American Journal of Comparative Law* 12, no. 1 (1963): 61–71.

———. "The Rule of What Law? A Korean Conundrum." *Journal of the International Commission of Jurists* 6, no. 2 (1965): 278–87.

———. *The Korean Political Tradition and Law: Essays in Korean Law and Legal History*. 2nd ed. Seoul: Hollym Corporation, 1971.

———. "The Affective Society: Values and Law in Korea." In *Korean Jurisprudence, Politics and Culture*, edited by Pyong-Choon Hahm, 282–317. Seoul: Yonsei University Press, 1986.

———. "The Decision Process in Korea." In *Korean Jurisprudence, Politics and Culture*, edited by Pyong-Choon Hahm, 95–121. Seoul: Yonsei University Press, 1986.

———. "Law and International Education Exchange: Vocational Training or Policy Science?" In *Korean Jurisprudence, Politics and Culture*, by Pyong-Choon Hahm, 524–28. Seoul: Yonsei University Press, 1986.

———. "A Study on the Korean Preference for Male Children." In *Korean Jurisprudence, Politics and Culture*, edited by Pyong-Choon Hahm, 213–40. Seoul: Yonsei University Press, 1986.

———. "Toward a New Theory of Korean Politics: A Reexamination of Traditional Factors." In *Korean Jurisprudence, Politics and Culture*, edited by Pyong-Choon Hahm, 252–81. Seoul: Yonsei University Press, 1986.

———. "The Traditional Patterns of Authoritative Symbols and the Judicial Process in Korea." In *Korean Jurisprudence, Politics and Culture*, edited by Pyong-Choon Hahm, 3–94. Seoul: Yonsei University Press, 1986.

Hahm, Pyong-Choon, and Byong-Je Jon. "The Criminality of Abortion in Korea." *Journal of Criminal Law and Criminology* 56, no. 1 (1965): 18–26.

Hahm, Pyong-Choon, Choong-Soon Kim, and Seung-Doo Yang. "Hangug Nodong-johab-ui Hyeonsilgwa Nodongbeob [Labor Law and the Reality of the Trade Unionism in Korea]." *Yonsei Nonchong* 3, no. 1 (1964): 213–50.

Hahm, Pyong-Choon, and Seung-Doo Yang. "The Attitudes of the Korean People Toward Law." In *Legal System of Korea*, edited by Shin-Yong Chun, 145–201. Seoul: International Cultural Foundations, 1975.

Hall, Jerome. *Living Law of Democratic Society*. Translated by Kyung-Hak Chang. Seoul: Eulyoo Publishing Co., 1960.

Han, Choong-Soo. "Sin-uichig-e Gihan Sogwon-ui Bagtalgwa Jeongjiui Jeongdang-seong Yeobue Gwanhayeo [Deprivation and Suspension of the Right of Action on the Basis of the Principle of Good Faith]." *Hanyang Law Review* 23, no. 1 (2006): 1–24.

Hart, H. L. A. *Essays on Bentham: Studies in Jurisprudence and Political Theory*. Oxford: Clarendon Press, 1982.

———. *Law, Liberty and Morality*. Translated by Young-Rahn Lee. Seoul: Nanam, 1996.

———. *The Concept of Law*. 2nd ed. Translated by Byung-Sun Oh. Seoul: Acanet, 2001.

Heise, Michael. "The Importance of Being Empirical." *Pepperdine Law Review* 26 (1999): 807–34.

Holmes, O. W. *The Common Law*. Translated by Kyung-Hak Chang. Seoul: Sudomunhwasa, 1962.

———. "The Path of the Law." *Harvard Law Review* 110, no. 5 (1997): 991–1009.

Ihm, Sahng-Hyeog. "Sosong Gipiui Munhwajeontong-e Daehan Jaegowa Hangugsahoe [Lawsuit Avoiding Tradition in East Asia and Reconsideration of It in Korean Society]." *Korean Journal of Law & Society* 25 (2003): 145–60.

Kim, Choong-Soon. "Hahm Pyong-Choon Seonsaengnim-ui Salmgwa Hagmun [Dr. Pyong-Choon Hahm: His Life and Scholarship]." *Yonsei Law Review* 24, no. 2 (2014): 1–20.

Kim, Dokyun. "Beob-wonliloseoui Gong-ig – Jayugonghwajuui Gong-iggwan-ui Sigag-eseo [Public Interest as a Legal Principle: A Liberal-Republican Conception of the Public Interest]." *Seoul Law Journal* 47, no. 3 (2006): 155–215.

———. "Seouldaehaggyo Beobhag 50-nyeon-eul Doedol-abomyeo: Beobcheolhag Bun-ya [Looking Back on 50 years of *Seoul Law Journal* – Philosophy of Law]." *Seoul Law Journal* 50, no. 2 (2009): 73–92.

———. "Uli Daebeob-won Beobhaeseoglon-ui Jeonhwan: Ronald Dworkin-ui Nun-eulo Ilg-gi – Beob-ui Tong-ilseong-eul Hyanghayeo [Taking Integrity Seriously: Recent Trends in the Jurisprudence of the Korean Supreme Court]." *Korean Journal of Legal Philosophy* 13, no. 1 (2010): 95–138.

Kim, Du-Eol. *Gyeongjeseongjang-gwa Sabeobjeongchaeg [Economic Growth and Judicial Policy]*. Seoul: Haenam Publishing, 2011.

Kim, Hyung-Suk. "Siljeungjuuiwa Gonglijuuiui Yeongyeol Goli – John Austin-ui Myeonglyeong-euloseoui Beob Gaenyeom [The Connection between Utilitarianism and Positivism – John Austin's Conception of Positive Law as Command]." *Hanyang Law Review* 36, no. 4 (2019): 451–92.

Kim, Jeong-Oh. "Jayujuui Beobchegyee Daehan Gujojeog Bunseoggwa Bipan – Deonkeon Kenediui Bipanbeobdamlon-eul Jungsim-eulo [Structural Analysis and Criticism of the Liberal Legal System]." *Yonsei Law Journal* 2 (1992): 653–82.

———. "Migug Bipanbeobhag-ui Heuleumgwa Donghyang [Trends of Critical Legal Studies in the US]." *Korean Journal of Law & Society* 10 (1994): 239–63.

———. "Bipanbeobhag-ui Woncheongwa Jaengjeomdeul [Sources and Issues of Critical Legal Studies]." In *Hyeondaebeobcheolhag-ui Heuleum [The Current of Legal Philosophy]*, edited by Korean Association of Legal Philosophy, 240–70. Seoul: Bobmunsa, 1996.

———. "Simin-ui Beobmunhwa (I): Beobmunhwaui Saeloun Insig [Citizens' Legal Culture (I): The New Perspective of Law and Culture]." *Yonsei Law Review* 8 (1998): 149–94.

———. "Roberto Unger-ui Sahoeilongwa Beob-ilon [Roberto Unger's Social Theory and Legal Theory]." *HUFS Law Review* 27 (2007): 615–51.

———. "Hahm Pyong-Choon Seonsaeng-ui Hangugbeobmunhwalon [Dr. Hahm Pyong-Choon's Thought on Korean Legal Culture]." *Yonsei Law Review* 24, no. 2 (2014): 21–58.

Kim, Jinhee et al. *EFA National Report: Republic of Korea*. Seoul: Korean National Commission for UNESCO, 2014.

Kim, Jong-Cheol. "Dicey-ui Beobsasang-gwa Jeongchisasang – Geu Sanghogwan-lyeonseong-e Jumoghayeo [The Legal Theory and Political Ideal of Albert Venn Dicey – with Special Reference to Their Relationship]." *Korean Journal of Legal Philosophy* 7, no. 2 (2004): 39–62.

Kim, Won-Yeol. "Yugyo Minjujuuiwa Gongdongche Yunligwan [The Confucian Democracy and the Viewpoint of Ethics on the Community]." *Epoch and Philosophy* 17, no. 3 (2006): 87–112.

Kim, Young-Whan. *Beobcheolhag-ui Geunbonmunje [Fundamental Issues of Legal Philosophy]*. Seoul: Hongmoonsa, 2012.

Korea Legislation Research Institute, ed. *Oegugbeob-ui Gyesuwa Beoblyeong-yong-eo [Reception of Foreign Laws and Terminology in Law]*. Seoul: KLRI, 2002.

———, ed. *Hangug Hyeondaebeobcheolhag-ui Hyeongseong-gwa Jeongae [The Forming and Unfolding of Contemporary Legal Philosophy in Korea]*. Seoul: Sechang Publishing Company, 2010.

Kwon, Kyung-Hwi, and Jeong-Oh Kim. "John Austin-ui Saeng-aewa Beobsasang [John Austin's Life and His Legal Thought]." *Korean Journal of Legal Philosophy* 21, no. 3 (2018): 89–128.

Langbroek, Philip, et al. "Methodology of Legal Research: Challenges and Opportunities." *Utrecht La Review* 13, no. 3 (2017): 1–8.

Lee, Chulwoo. "Talking about Korean Legal Culture: A Critical Review of the Discursive Production of Legal Culture in Korea." *Korea Journal* 38, no. 3 (1998): 45–76.

———. "Legal Culture and the Rule of Law in Korea." *Hanyang Law Review* 16 (1999): 385–404.

———. "Beobmunhwaui Damlonjeog Saengsan: Bangbeoblonjeog Bipan [The Discursive Production of Legal Culture: A Methodological Critique]." *Korean Journal of Legal Philosophy* 14, no. 1 (2001): 203–30.

———. "Editor's Note: Yonsei Remembers Hahm Pyong-Choon." *Yonsei Law Journal* 4, no. 2 (2013): 113–18.

———. "Hahm Pyong-Choon Gyosu (1932–1983): Jeontong, Geundae, Segyeui Gyochajeom-eseo Beob-eul Malhada [Professor Pyong-Choon Hahm (1932~1983): To Speak the Law at the Intersection of Tradition, Modernity and the World]." In *Yeonsei-ui Beobhagjadeul* I *[Legal Scholars of Yonsei* I*]*, edited by Jong-Soo Lee et al., 163–212. Seoul: Yonsei University Press, 2020.

Lee, Kuk-Woon. "19-segi Yeong-gug-ui Bunseogbeobhag – John Austin-ui Beob-ilon-eul Jungsim-eulo [Analytical Jurisprudence in 19th Century Britain]." *Korean Journal of Legal Philosophy* 3, no. 2 (2000): 35–64.

Lee, Kye Il. "'Silje Sog-ui Beob' Gwannyeom-eul Jungsim-eulo Bon Hyeonsiljuui Beob-ilon-ui Byeoncheon [Transformation of Realistic Legal Theory: Focus on the Conception of 'Law in Action']." *Yonsei Law Review* 20, no. 1 (2010): 146–87.

Lee, Sang-Young. "Bentham-ui Beobgaenyeomgwa Ibbeoblon-e Daehan Sogo [The Study on the Concept of Law and the Theory Legislation]." *World Constitutional Law Review* 13, no. 2 (2007): 149–94.

———. "Bentham-ui Common Law Chegyee Daehan Bipangwa Ibbeoblon Gusang-e Daehan Yeongu [A Search for New Perspectives on Judicial Precedent: A Study about the Criticism on the Common Law System and the Construction of Theory of Legislation]." *Seoul Law Journal* 49, no. 3 (2008): 1–39.

———. "Gonglijuui Dae Jayeongwon [Theory of Utilitarianism versus Natural Rights]." *World Constitutional Law Review* 16, no. 2 (2010): 295–334.

———. "Sabeob Dae Ibbeob – Bentham-ui 'Pannomion (Wanjeonhan Beobchegye)'e Daehan Yeongu ['Adjudication' versus 'Legislation' – Under J. Bentham's 'Pannomion']." *Ilkam Law Review* 21 (2012): 557–612.

———. "J. Bentham-ui Segyeheonbeob Gusang-e Daehan Sogo – Segye Gongtong Heonbeob? [A Study on Bentham's Conception of the Constitutional Law of the World – A Common Constitutional Law?]." *Ajou Law Research* 8, no. 3 (2014): 145–78.

———. "J. Bentham 'Heonbeobjeon'eseoui Ibbeobbue Daehan Yeongu: 'Segyegongtongheonbeob'eseoui Ibbeobbuui Gineung, Gwonhan, Geuligo Guseong-eun Eotteohge Doel Geos-inga [A Study on the Legislature in Bentham's Constitutional Code: Power, Function, and Structure of the Legislature in Bentham's Constitutional Code]." *Legislation and Policy Studies* 8, no. 2 (2016): 167–92.

———. "Gonglijuuijaui Heonbeobjeon Yeongu – J. Bentham-ui 'Heonbeobjeon'ui Guseong-gwa Teugjing [A Study on the Utilitarian Constitutional Code – Aspects and Figures of Bentham's 'Constitutional Code']." *Inha Law Review* 19, no. 3 (2016): 213–51.

McDougal, Myres S. "Jurisprudence for a Free Society." *Georgia Law Review* 1, no. 1 (1966): 1–19.

Moon, Joon-Young. *Beob-wongwa Geomchal-ui Tansaeng [The Birth of the Court and the Prosecution]*. Seoul: Yuksabipyeongsa, 2010.

Oh, Byung-Sun. "Hart-ui Beobcheolhag Bangbeobgwa Beob-ui Gaenyeom [H.L.A. Hart's Method of Jurisprudence and the Concept of Law]." In *Hyeondaebeobcheolhag-ui Heuleum [The Current of Legal Philosophy]*, edited by Korean Association of Legal Philosophy, 21–47. Seoul: Bobmunsa, 1996.

———. "Ryu Kichyun-ui Beobsasang [Legal Thoughts of Paul K. Ryu]." In *Dasi Ryu Kichyun-eul Saeng-Gaghanda [Rethinking Paul K. Ryu]*, edited by The Paul K. Ryu Foundation, 179–203. Seoul: Bobmunsa, 2015.

Pak, Pyong-Ho. *Geunse-ui Beobgwa Beobsasang [Law and Legal Thoughts of Modern Ages]*. Seoul: Jinwon, 1996.

Pak, Un-Jong. "Bangbeobsajeog Gwanjeom-eseo Bon Hobbes-ui Jayeonbeobsasang [Thomas Hobbes' Thinking about Natural Law – Methodological Consideration]." *Korea Cultural Research Institute Nonchong* 49 (1986): 363–80.

———. "Gihahag-ui Jeongsingwa Geundaejayeonbeob [The Spirit of Geometry and the Modern Law of Nature]." *Ewha Journal of Social Sciences* 6 (1986): 3–14.

———. "Yeoseongjuuiwa Bipanjeog Beob-ilon [Feminism and Critical Legal Theory]." In *Hyeondaebeobcheolhag-ui Heuleum [The Current of Legal Philosophy]*, edited by Korean Association of Legal Philosophy, 271–322. Seoul: Bobmunsa, 1996.

———. "Beobgwangwa Beobcheolhag [The Judge and Legal Philosophy]." *Seoul Law Journal* 53, no. 1 (2012): 299–324.

———. "Beobhaeseogbangbeob-eseo Bon Heonbeob Je-103-jo Beobgwan-ui Doglibgwa Yangsim [The Independence and Conscience of Judges Based on the Interpretive Method for Article 103 of the Korean Constitution]." *Seoul Law Journal* 57, no. 2 (2016): 63–103.

Park, Il-Kyung. "Hobbes-wa Locke-e Iss-eoseoui Ingwon [Human Rights in Hobbes and Locke]." *Bubjo* 17, no. 8 (1968): 1–12.

Park, Joon-Seok. *Beobsasang, Saeng-gaghal Uimue Daehayeo [Making Law Intelligible: Essays in Legal Ideas]*. Seoul: Acanet, 2015.

Park, Kwang-Seo. "Siljeungjuuibeobhag-ui Seongu (J. Austin) [A Precursor of Legal Positivism (J. Austin)]." In *Geundaebeobsasang-ui Jeongae [The Unfolding of Modern Legal Thought: Festschrift for Dr. Gyung-Hak Chang]*, edited by Publication Committee, 105–17. Seoul: Shinheung Printing Co., Ltd., 1977.

Pound, Roscoe. "Law in Books and Law in Action." *American Law Review* 44 (1910): 12–36.
———. *The Spirit of the Common Law*. Translated by Chung-Han Kim. Seoul: Minjungseogwan, 1950.
———. *The Task of Law*. Translated by Hyo-Young Kim and Ih-Jun Ahn. Seoul: Wiseongmunhwasa, 1955.
———. *Interpretations of Legal History*. Translated by Byeong-Guk Go. Seoul: Ilhan Publishing Co., 1956.
———. *New Paths of the Law*. Translated by Byeong-Guk Go and Bum-Chan Lee. Seoul: Bobmunsa, 1958.
———. *Justice According to Law*. Translated by Ton-Kak Suh. Seoul: Bobmunsa, 1959.
———. *An Introduction to the Philosophy of Law*. Translated by Hang-Neyong Yi and Yeo-Su Kim. Seoul: Jungumsa, 1960.
Rostow, Eugene V. "Myres S. McDougal." *The Yale Law Journal* 84 (1975): 704–17.
Ryu, Paul K. "Causation in Criminal Law." *University of Pennsylvania Law Review* 106, no. 6 (1958): 773–805.
———. *Gaejeong Hyeongbeobhag (Chonglongang-ui)* [*Criminal Law: Lectures on General Provisions*]. Facsimile ed. Seoul: Bobmunsa, 2011.
———. *Korean Culture and Criminal Responsibility*. Seoul: Bobmunsa, 2011.
———. "Beobgwa Pyeonghwa [Law and Peace]." In *Jayusahoeui Beobgwa Jeong-ui [Law and Justice in a Free Society]*, edited by The Paul K. Ryu Foundation, 79–96. Seoul: Bobmunsa, 2015.
The Paul K. Ryu Foundation, ed. *Dasi Ryu Kichyun-eul Saeng-Gaghanda [Rethinking Paul K. Ryu]*. Seoul: Bobmunsa, 2015.
Ryu, Paul K., and Helen Silving. "Towards a Rational System of Criminal Law." *Seoul Law Journal* 4 (1962): 2–24.
———. "Was bedeutet die sogenannte 'Relativität der Rechtsbegriffe'?" *ARSP* 59, no. 1 (1973): 57–96.
Shim, Hun-Sup. "Beob-ui Hyolyeog-e Gwanhan Yeongu [Investigations into the Validity of the Law]." *Seoul Law Journal* 21, no. 1 (1980): 141–73.
———. "Beobgaenyeom-e Gwanhan Non-ui [Discussions on the Concept of Law]." *Seoul Law Journal* 31, no. 1 & 2 (1990): 61–72.
———. "Beobgwa Dodeog-ui Gwangye [On the Relationship between Law and Morals]." *Seoul Law Journal* 18, no. 1 (1977): 226–36.
———. "Bipanjeog Beobsiljeungjuui [Critical Legal Positivism]." In *Hyeondaesahoegwahagbangbeoblon [Methods of Modern Social Science]*, edited by Korea Social Science Institute, 151–69. Seoul: Minumsa, 1977.
———. "H.L.A. Hart-ui Bunseogjeog Beob-ilon [H.L.A. Hart's Analytical Jurisprudence]." *SabeobHaengjeong* 19, no. 3 (1978): 48–54.
———. "Gwon-wie Gwanhayeo – Baejejeog Beobsiljeungjuuieseo Poyongjeog Beobsiljeungjuuielo [About Authority]." *Seoul Law Journal* 39, no. 2 (1998): 103–23.
Shim, Zai-Woo. "Thomas Hobbes-ui Beobsasang [Legal Thought of Thomas Hobbes]." In *Beobsasang-gwa Minsabeob [Legal Thought and Civil Law: Festschrift for Dr. Seung-Jong Hyeon]*, edited by Publication Committee, 61–83. Seoul: Kookminbooks Co., Ltd., 1979.
Shin, Dong-Ryong. "Jayujuuijeog Jeojaggwon Damlon-ui Seong-gwawa Hangyee Daehan Gochal [The Contributions and Limits of the Liberal Copyright Theory]." *Korean Journal of Legal Philosophy* 8, no. 1 (2005): 113–50.

Shin, Dongwoon. "Hyeongbeob Je20jo Sahoesang-gyu Gyujeong-ui Seonglib-gyeong-wi [Korean Criminal Act (Article 20)]." *Seoul Law Journal* 47, no. 2 (2006): 189–219.
Shin, Dongwoon et al. *Beoblyulhaeseog-ui Hangye [The Limit of Statutory Interpretation]*. Seoul: Bobmunsa, 2000.
Silbey, Susan. "After Legal Consciousness." *Annual Review of Law and Social Science* 1 (2005): 323–68.
Tjon, Uon-Bae. "Agbeob-ui Beobli – Agbeobgyujun-e Iss-eoseoui Beobsiljeungju-uiwa Beob-uisig-ui Gineung [On the Principle of Evil Law]." *Seoul Law Journal* 11, no. 1 (1969): 5–34.
Tyler, Tom R. "Methodology in Legal Research." *Utrecht Law Review* 13, no. 3 (2017): 130–41.
Yang, Chun-Soo. "Sangjingjuui Hyeongbeob-ilon: Ryu Kichyun Gyosuui Hyeongbe-obcheolhag [The Theory of Symbolic Criminal Law: Paul K. Ryu's Philosophy of Criminal Law]." *Korean Journal of Law & Society* 64 (2020): 103–42.
Yang, Kun. "Migug Beobsasang-eseoui Geubjinjuuijeog Heuleum [Radical Trends in American Legal Thought]." *American Studies* 8 (1985): 1–12.
———. "Hangug-eseoui 'Beobgwa Sahoe' Yeongu [The 'Law and Society' Studies in Korea]." *Korean Journal of Law & Society* 1 (1989): 66–83.
———. "The Law and Society Studies in Korea: Beyond the Hahm Theses." *Law & Society Review* 23, no. 5 (1989): 891–902.
Yen, Chueh-An. "Normative Gap, Subjugation and Recognition." *Proceedings of the XXII World Congress of Philosophy* 40 (2008): 185–94.
Yoon, Se-Chang. "Beob-ui Jibaeui Beobli (A.V. Dicey) [Principle of the Rule of Law (A.V. Dicey)]." In *Geundaebeobsasang-ui Jeongae* [*The Unfolding of Modern Legal Thought: Festschrift for Dr. Gyung-Hak Chang*], edited by Publication Committee, 118–34. Seoul: Shinheung Printing Co., Ltd., 1977.
Yoon, Zai-Wang. "Gaeinjuuijeog Jeoldaejuui – Thomas Hobbes-ui Guggacheolhag-gwa Beobcheolhag-e Gwanhayeo [Individualistic Absolutism: About the Philosophy of Law and State of Thomas Hobbes]." *Journal of Law Research* 28, no. 2 (2012): 7–36.

Constitutional Court Decision 2002Hun-Ma518 Decided October 30, 2003.
Supreme Court Decision 82Do357 Decided February 8, 1983.
Supreme Court en banc Decision 94Mo32 Decided December 20, 1994.
Seoul District Court Decision 99Gahap30782 Decided January 16, 2001.

Conclusion

Jeong-Oh Kim

As a product of intellectual studies and scholarly arguments, the philosophy of law is not thought to impact social reality directly. The development of Korean legal philosophy reveals a different picture. Over the past seventy years, Korean scholars have accepted Western legal philosophy while advancing their thoughts and evaluating legal philosophy's role in Korean society.

Until the 1980s, Korea's modern legal system was not properly established, and legal philosophical research was not sufficiently developed. Nonetheless, ideas of democracy, human rights, and the rule of law, rooted in the Western legal tradition, attracted young students, and provided a strong foundation for their views. When serious legal issues arose and fierce debates ensued in the 1990s, Korean legal philosophers corrected distorted arguments by presenting more accurate and persuasive interpretations of Western legal theories. Though small steps, their intellectual efforts aided the judiciary in hard cases.

Returning to William Twining's arguments raised in the introduction, we should use the Korean experience to rethink the distinction between global and parochial jurisprudence. Twining asked,

> Where concepts such as court or constitution or corruption or lawyer have deep roots in local history or have acquired strong cultural or ideological baggage, the dangers of ethnocentric projection are obvious. So it is worth asking, how much of our stock of concepts is local and context-specific?[1]

Although Twining presents the problem of locality that the Western legal system implies and emphasizes its globalization, he does not provide a case where a country suffered serious problems from importing a Western legal system. The United Kingdom and the United States belong to the common law system, and France and Germany belong to the civil law system, but each has built a legal system peculiar to its history and society. Rather than a unified objective entity, Western legal systems share ideas – democracy, liberty, equality, human rights, and the rule of law – that they seek to realize through various types of legal regulations and institutions. Similarly, Korean legal scholars, including legal philosophers, have worked very hard to realize democracy and human rights because

DOI: 10.4324/9781003156437-5

they believed those values suited and enhanced Korea's polity and society, not to replicate some objective Western legal system.

Thus, the Korean experience described in this book demonstrates that Twining's question will be answered differently according to the situation in which the Western legal system is accepted. Countries will approach this heterogeneity differently, and intellectuals in countries that have accepted the Western system will seriously explore how to overcome and integrate heterogeneity.

During Japan's colonization of Korea, Japanese authorities accepted a Western legal system, incorporated it into their legal system, and applied it to Korean society. Though Koreans felt a great sense of heterogeneity, they did not seek to resolve the disparity or adapt themselves to it. However, after liberation in 1945, Koreans established a Western legal system and seriously considered the heterogeneity between that system and their traditional culture.

As we have seen in Chapters 1 and 3, this issue was one of the main tasks that Korean legal scholars sought to resolve in the 1960s. At that time, the primary reason for their in-depth exploration of the relationship between Korean traditional culture and a transplanted modern legal system was not academic interest but a social reality where this gap significantly hindered social development. Most leaders also saw this as an obstacle.

Addressing this situation in the 1960s, Pyong-Choon Hahm stated,

> In discussing the problems of transplanting a modern legal system, the underlying assumption has invariably been that such an action is unavoidable. Another assumption is that since Roman law 'worked' in the case of the Germanic peoples in Europe, there is no reason why the same should not be true with Asians and Africans. Apart from the validity of the assertion concerning Roman law in Europe, the analogy between Europe and Asia seems false. The imported legal system has not 'worked' in Korea. It has remained an alien system confined to urban centers. It has failed to make itself relevant, let alone indispensable, to the life of the majority of the population. The indigenous way of life is so different from the European way of life, out of which the imported legal system had grown, that the wonder is it has not caused more disruption and disorganization. The predicament faced by Korea is that the norms of positive law not only lack the support of 'the normative customs of the living law' but the two conflict with each other.
>
> It is therefore imperative that the conflict between the imported legal system and the indigenous jural values of the people should be at least minimized. One solution would be to reject the imported system and revert to the traditional system. This appears, however, impossible in view of the existing commitment to modernization on the part of the political leadership. Moreover, rapidly increasing international interdependence, especially international trade, rules out such a possibility. Another solution would be to go to the opposite extreme and ruthlessly root out the traditional values. But the mores have proven themselves extremely resilient. Such a course of action would only intensify the conflict. It is therefore necessary to accept the fact of conflict and do our best to minimize it.[2]

Hahm understood that this discrepancy could be resolved from a future-oriented perspective rather than merely a retrospective method. Furthermore, he recognized that the two systems are indispensable for the future of Korean society, and he accepted as his main task finding a way to combine them creatively. Hahm's fundamental dilemma was that the creative union between two heterogeneous systems was rare. He understood that to promote the modernization of Korean society and establish a more rational Western legal system, Korea had no choice but to discard the indigenous traditions rooted in the society. More importantly, the West's modern legal system is not something that can be superficially adopted, like wearing Western-style clothes. It requires changing the values that govern all human relationships, including the Koreans' worldview. Hahm defined such a process as a perennial problematic.[3]

In some sense, it is true that the locality rooted in Western legal systems and thought, suggested by Twining, causes significant problems for non-Western societies. However, this psychological confusion cannot be solved by the Westerners who established the system; rather, the burden and responsibility rest on the people who actively accept it. Korean history and society represent this process and reveal its difficulty.

It seems that conflicts between the Westernized legal system and traditional culture, and efforts to close those gaps, have occurred at several layers in society. We saw two layers when we looked at the development of Korean legal philosophy.

One layer is guided by the desires and actions of a community to create a society for a more humane life, leading to social change. The ideal conceptions and institutions created by the Western legal system, such as human dignity, human rights, liberty, democracy, and the rule of law, are the driving forces for social change, although the institutions that specifically realize those ideas have not been established. As described in Chapter 1, they operated as an important indicator in the struggle of young people and intellectuals against the authoritarian government during the 1960s, and as a spiritual indicator in which more citizens could participate. Through these movements, ideals spread and permeated the consciousness of people who had not directly engaged in the anti-government struggle. This process contributed to solving the heterogeneity between the Western legal system and traditional culture.

The second layer influencing heterogeneity between the two systems can be found in the process of social and economic change. Korea's economic development, which started in the 1960s, brought tremendous social transformation, such as rapid, enormous population growth and shifts in the economic system, market structure, living environment, and family composition. These changes in social conditions have brought about significant changes in Koreans' consciousness and behavior regarding norms, order, and emotions.[4]

Dai-Kwon Choi, a legal sociologist, described the features of Korea's rural villages in the mid-1970s,

> A village forms a unit of dispute resolution, and it is the traditional norm that fights in a family should not go outside the home and fights in a neighborhood should not go outside the village. Criminal cases such as drunken

> assault or theft rarely occur in the village, but, if such an event occurs, it is resolved through the process of compensation, apology, reconciliation, and concession within the village. Rarely are these cases pending at the police station. Even if that happens, they are usually resolved by the local police officer or the villagers before being handed over to police headquarters.[5]

This description shows the characteristics of a traditional Korean rural village. Such a dispute resolution process was closely related to the structure of rural villages at that time, which emphasized human relationships among its members. This traditional communal life maintains considerable autonomy in terms of norms. The villages have the normative autonomy to resolve disputes or address deviant behaviors occurring in the village rather than entrust them to outsiders or institutions. The dispute is not left to a court judge or a third party completely unfamiliar with the villagers but is resolved by neighbors or other adults in the village who know the victim and perpetrator.

This method of dispute resolution is completely different from the contemporary process. The traditional normative community is very similar to the picture of a community described by Alasdair MacIntyre, a communitarian philosopher.[6] The peculiarity of the traditional communities is that their norms were rooted in human bonds. The norms of conduct and communal ties depend on the morality and value system shared by the villagers. The formation and maintenance of the community are deeply rooted in human reciprocity and solidarity.

However, the traditional normative community has its limits. First, the personality and desires of an individual living in the community are restricted to a considerable degree. It is not easy for a resident to act differently from neighbors or hold different values because the community norms were formed homogeneously. Second, the effectiveness of community norms is limited. The norms apply only to village members, not those who belong to other communities. It seems that communal norms contain double standards. For example, it is easy to tolerate a villager's delinquency or violation of norms, but outsiders cannot expect this tolerance.

A normative community can be maintained when the same people live together in the same place for a long time. However, the tremendous second layer changes that have taken place in Korea make it nearly impossible for the normative community to be maintained. It seems that the modern legal system will replace a broken traditional normative community, overcoming the heterogeneity between the traditional norm system and the modern legal system in Korean society.

When we see the changing normative system and legal culture, it is not easy to understand the distinction between global and parochial jurisprudence in only geographical terms. Even if a legal system is formed in one region, other populations may adopt and incorporate its worthwhile ideas and system. Looking at the changes in the first layer, when Koreans accepted concepts, such as human dignity, human rights, liberty, democracy, and the rule of law, that are embedded in the Western legal system, it seems that those concepts lost their locality and parochiality, going beyond those thresholds to the dimension of universality.

Korea's modern legal philosophy has actively accepted and developed through Western philosophies. However, this was proceeded by Korean legal philosophers' ceaseless efforts and interactions with Western scholarship while also considering Korea's political and social contexts. Likewise, the Korean experience described by our authors can broaden the horizon of Western legal philosophy.

Notes

1 William Twining, *General Jurisprudence: Understanding Law from a Global Perspective* (Cambridge: Cambridge University Press, 2009), 61–62.
2 Pyong-Choon Hahm, *Korean Jurisprudence, Politics and Culture* (Seoul: Yonsei University Press, 1986), 153.
3 Jeong-Oh Kim, *Hangug-ui Beobmunhwa: Insig, Gujo, Byeonhwa [Korean Legal Culture: Understanding, Structure and Change]* (Seoul: Nanam, 2006), 29–41.
4 Ibid., 154.
5 Dai-Kwon Choi, *Beobsahoehag [Sociology of Law]* (Seoul, Seoul National University Press, 1986), 158.
6 Alasdair MacIntyre, *After Virtue: A Study in Moral Theory*, trans. Jin-Woo Lee (Seoul: Moonye Publishing Co., 1997), 324.

Bibliograhpy

Choi, Dai-Kwon. *Beobsahoehag [Sociology of Law]*. Seoul: Seoul National University Press, 1986.

Hahm, Pyong-Choon. *Korean Jurisprudence, Politics and Culture*. Seoul: Yonsei University Press, 1986.

Kim, Jeong-Oh. *Hangug-ui Beobmunhwa: Insig, Gujo, Byeonhwa [Korean Legal Culture: Understanding, Structure and Change]*. Seoul: Nanam, 2006.

MacIntyre, Alasdair. *After Virtue: A Study in Moral Theory*. Translated by Jin-Woo Lee. Seoul: Moonye Publishing Co., 1997.

Twining, William. *General Jurisprudence: Understanding Law from a Global Perspective*. Cambridge: Cambridge University Press, 2009.

Index

For Product Safety Concerns and Information please contact our EU representative GPSR@taylorandfrancis.com
Taylor & Francis Verlag GmbH, Kaufingerstraße 24, 80331 München, Germany

www.ingramcontent.com/pod-product-compliance
Ingram Content Group UK Ltd.
Pitfield, Milton Keynes, MK11 3LW, UK
UKHW022314250926
475702UK00046B/777
* 9 7 8 0 3 6 7 7 4 1 7 8 5 *